T0158056

THE MIND OF THE INDIVIDUAL

THE MIND OF THE INDIVIDUAL

MY AUTOBIOGRAPHY BY

BEVERLY CUFFY

iUniverse, Inc.
Bloomington

The Mind of the Individual
My Autobiography

Copyright © 2011 by Beverly Cuffy.

All rights reserved. No part of this book may be used or reproduced by any means, graphic, electronic, or mechanical, including photocopying, recording, taping or by any information storage retrieval system without the written permission of the publisher except in the case of brief quotations embodied in critical articles and reviews.

No part of this book may be reproduced or transferred in any form or by any means, graphic, electronic, or mechanical, including photocopying, recording, taping, or by any information storage retrieval system, without the permission of the author.

The accuracy and completeness of information provided herein and opinions stated herein are not guaranteed or warranted to produce any particular results, and the advice and strategies, contained herein may not be suitable for every individual.

The author shall not be liable for any loss incurred as a consequence of the use and application, directly or indirectly, of any information presented in this work. This publication is designed to provide accuracy in regard to the subject matter covered. The author has used her efforts in preparing this book. Sold with the understanding, that the author is not engaged in professional services.

iUniverse books may be ordered through booksellers or by contacting:

iUniverse
1663 Liberty Drive
Bloomington, IN 47403
www.iuniverse.com
1-800-Authors (1-800-288-4677)

Because of the dynamic nature of the Internet, any web addresses or links contained in this book may have changed since publication and may no longer be valid. The views expressed in this work are solely those of the author and do not necessarily reflect the views of the publisher, and the publisher hereby disclaims any responsibility for them.

Any people depicted in stock imagery provided by Thinkstock are models, and such images are being used for illustrative purposes only.
Certain stock imagery © Thinkstock.

ISBN: 978-1-4620-6222-5 (sc)
ISBN: 978-1-4620-6224-9 (hc)
ISBN: 978-1-4620-6223-2 (ebk)

Printed in the United States of America

iUniverse rev. date: 1/4/2012

This book is dedicated to my mother who taught me to believe that all things are possible.

CONTENTS

PREFACE

Many years ago when I began teaching I realised my love for books extended beyond reading; and I hoped one day I would be a writer. I wrote a few short stories over the years, but so far have remained unpublished.

The ideas for my autobiography began some fifteen years ago when I knew I wanted to write something about my family. I felt I needed to correct certain misconceptions and that writing my own life story might prove one way of ensuring accuracy in my family history.

In March 2011, I finally found the motivation that was required to write my autobiography. I was in St Vincent & the Grenadines at the time. My family are originally from that country and I have remaining relatives on the island. I am a single person and am aware that sometimes the truth is distorted or changed during the passage of time. Given this is the case I recognised the need to point out the injustices in my own life; as well as ensure that my parents true characters were reflected and regained their original status as good, honourable and loving people.

I mention this because of a comment which was made by a complete stranger last year (2010), the comment was: "Your mother has been disrespected for years; and I have no wish for similar comments to be made for mine." This highlighted that the project had wider implications than I had first understood. It was important that it was written not just for me, and future generations to gain some historical truths, but also to ensure a retraction of the repeated inaccurate and at times disgusting comments about my mother.

Further repeats of previously recorded information as well as current comments being the subject of court action, as required.

I have written this book bearing in mind my own personal circumstances, and taking into account the cycle of abuse which is on-going in my life. I have also written this book with consideration and an awareness of others who may have experienced similar difficulties. My objective in sharing this story is that it might be enlightening and offer hope for others.

I have encouraged the reader to compare and contrast some of the experiences described with those of characters in certain pieces of literature. I believe this will make the work less introspective and appeal to a wider audience. The project was put on hold for a short time because I had certain other priorities which needed attending to prior to writing my memoirs. Thus it wasn't until August 2011 on my return from England that I finally began to put my thoughts down on paper. I found a quiet place in St John, USVI where I could write in a fairly undisturbed manner.

We are all unique, and are shaped by our life experiences. I believe that my story is interesting and should be shared because it clearly describes in powerful language the abuse which I have endured for almost a decade.

ACKNOWLEDGEMENTS

In my autobiography I have spent a lot of time discussing the negative aspects of my life, and would now like to acknowledge those who were supportive of me during the difficult times. No man is an island, and I know that I could never have gotten through this horrendous period without the support of those who I know wish to remain nameless. They are not forgotten and I extend my heartfelt gratitude-you all know who you are.

Those of my siblings who were involved in supporting me during this time, either by offering financial support or asking those who were supporting me to continue, I would like to take this opportunity of thanking them for the emotional and financial assistance which was given.

Also during this time two family members, Barbara Palmer and Ken Cox who were much loved and greatly appreciated,

Beverly Cuffy

passed away and I just wanted to take this opportunity of remembering them.

Finally, I would like to thank my editors

INTRODUCTION

As a black woman writing my autobiography I researched other autobiographical writings prior to writing my own. There are many writings which could be cited as having echoes with my life or could be juxtaposed. I have chosen to look at the first autobiographical writings of Maya Angelou who has been my heroine for many years. I find her work both inspirational and encouraging and believe the subjects covered in much of her work clearly identify some of the themes which I have attempted to cover in this book. The themes in '*I know why the Caged Bird Sings*' are a celebration of motherhood, a critique of racism, the importance of family, the quest for independence, personal dignity and self-definition. In addition I have included the novel '*The Color Purple*' by Alice Walker which also discusses the subject of abuse from a woman's perspective and illustrates the notion of sisterhood.[1]

I believe quite strongly that most mothers deserve a medal. I have a real affinity and love for those who have nurtured us through our formative years, and recognise the importance of a mother. Although I am not a mother, I had one, who was very genuine, kind and loving. I personally believe her memory should remain intact as an inspiration to all she came into contact with. As such I am using this novel as a way of celebrating her and in ensuring her memory is seen positively and not denigrated. My mother was a good person who in addition to her six children took in many who were experiencing difficulty in their own home. She was an informal foster mother to many, a confidante, and a caring and supportive parent whose prime aim was to nurture her young and encourage us to believe in ourselves. The only way she should be regarded is in these terms and any inappropriate personal references are to be disregarded from hereon in. I believe throughout this book I have given an indication of how important she is to all of her family, and how distressing it is to learn that she has in anyway been disrespected. This is undeserved and I would ask that previously recorded comments be disregarded as inaccurate and untrue.

As well as the importance of motherhood this autobiography clearly documents racism as it affected our lives in the early 1970s. During this period there were certain immigration laws, and proponents of nationalism in Britain who believed that black people should be deported back to their country of origin. This school of thought was evident in the education system, and whilst we were not deported, we were certainly discouraged from attaining educational success. This is alluded to in my discussion of my early years at secondary school when I mention that I was discouraged from staying on at school and getting formal qualifications which would guarantee getting a good job with prospects. Instead I, like other students whose parents were from the Caribbean, were steered towards working in a factory. It is because my parents valued education to such a high degree and insisted that I went onto further education that I eventually realised that I enjoyed studying; and this finally prompted me to take further qualifications.

In addition to the above subjects I have within this novel discussed in some depth the relationship which I currently have with my siblings, and identified one particular sibling relationship which is especially fraught with difficulties. This discussion is off-set by the way in which our parents encouraged us to be supportive and love one another.

A central motif within this autobiography is abuse. This discussion ranges from the personal abuse experienced by myself to a more general discussion of abuse and its psychological effects. I still fall asleep in the middle of the day after being pulverized for weeks and being systematically woken up. This leaves me vulnerable to abuse, both sexual and physical. When this is the case I find my strength in God. Although some might consider me to be something of a 'Pollyanna' it is the way in which I view the world which has prompted me to believe in myself and encouraged me to take up where necessary self-help techniques. A more general discussion of abuse is identified by considering the effects of those who for whatever reason find themselves being bullied, intimidated and treated differently.

I have still to escape the confines and shackles of those who in some way seem to believe that they should take ownership of my life, but where there is life there is hope.

CHAPTER ONE

ABOUT THE AUTHOR

Monday 15th August 2011

Robert L Bradshaw Airport, St Kitts

LIAT the airline used in the Caribbean is late. I awoke early to catch the flight which should have left the island at 8.30 am. It's now 11.00 am and they have just announced that the plane is going to be late, perhaps leaving the island at 11.40 or thereabouts. St Kitts and Nevis like most of the islands in the Caribbean is quite beautiful and full of white sandy beaches. It is currently being developed and some of the homes when completed will be both beautiful and costly. The family house is on the island and I've checked that any outstanding bills are paid. It's a sunny day with a light zephyr wafting over us. The AC isn't turned on, and as the few early morning passengers gradually begin to increase, the sound of voices and background music can be heard more audibly and distinctly. This was a short visit, only ten days to transact my business. As the plane was late I thought this seemed as good a time as any to begin my autobiography. I am on my way to Tortola, BVI in search of a place to settle and call home.

It's been well documented that writing about one's self can be therapeutic, either that or very narcissistic. I am not anyone famous, so why should I write about my life, well amidst the gossip and stories made up about me, I felt it was important for posterity that an accurate interpretation of the happenings in my life were available, should anyone ever want another perspective.

It was instilled in us from childhood, my siblings and I, that in order to be successful in life you needed to study hard. My parents like many first generation West Indian immigrants placed an enormous amount of importance on education. I was taught to believe that once you achieved or attained academic success you could do whatever you chose. As I grew older I learned this was not always the case. There are those who always need to be in control; and those who feel the need to assert power. I see this as insecurity in their own lives; this need to control or appear to control has to be a lack of something in themselves or their lives.

I suppose I am something of an observer of other people and their lives. They are certainly very keen to gossip and repeat what they think they know about mine. Perhaps I should start at the beginning, where exactly is that? Well I suppose it began with my birth. This is not a fairy story it's a true story, one which I hope you enjoy reading.

I was born on the 5th January 1955 at Lagos Hospital, Oranjestad, Aruba, and later christened Beverly Veronica

Cuffy. My parents were Harold Caulton Ethan Cuffy, who was born on the 31st August 1922 and died on 19th January 1985. My mother was Eileen Veronica Cuffy (nee Williams) who was born on 4th March 1922 and who sadly left us on 10th November 1993. My father was born in Georgetown, St Vincent and my mother was born in Basseterre, St Kitts. My parents met and married in Aruba, where they had both emigrated in order to enhance their economic prospects. I was a bold child and remember my mother proudly discussing a recitation I gave at the tender age of 3 years. She said I spoke in a loud, booming voice; I was a very confident child.

I am the fourth child of Harold and Eileen and the fairest in terms of skin colouring. This led to a friend and neighbour ascribing me as the child of the local fisherman, who was called 'Stones'. He would forcibly argue, if with a lot of laughter and amusement that my father had been duped. Essentially the jest would be similar to the English joke that the child belonged to the milkman.

I attended the local nursery school and enjoyed learning. I also enjoyed playing in the red dirt as a child. I have several early childhood memories one of which is attending school with one of my older sisters. It was a Christmas party, and surprisingly they had a Santa Claus who kept throwing sweets into the crowd of children. I was very young, perhaps three or four years old, and couldn't seem to catch any. I remember being quite upset by this, and to console me my sister gave me some of hers. I have five sisters and one brother. Meredith who is the eldest is six years my senior. She's about 5'4 "in height, brown skinned and medium build. The second eldest is Alexandrena who is four years my senior. She's approximately 5'3", very slender and of a similar complexion to myself. The third eldest of my siblings is Venetta who is three years older than I. She's approximately 5'3", of a medium brown complexion and of medium build. Yvonne, my half-sister is approximately 5'4", her complexion is a light brown and she is seven years older than I. Thecla is the youngest of the girls and is approximately 5'3" in height. She's of a medium brown complexion and two years my junior. The youngest child of my parents is Brian who is four years younger than myself. He is fairly dark in complexion, about 5'10" in height and heavily built. I also had two half-brothers, Ken and Keith who lived for the most part in North America. Although they lived in another country I was fortunate to meet both of them on several occasions before they passed away.

We immigrated to England from Aruba in 1960, and initially rented a few rooms from a lady from the Caribbean. A few months later my parents bought their own house, 11A Avenue Crescent, Leeds 8. This is the home that I grew up in amidst some poverty, much fun and a great deal of love. A lot of the fun can be ascribed to being a part of the Aruban community who were an integral part of my life. I say this because I grew up as part of an extended group of people from Aruba who were living in Leeds. These were the friends of my parents who became the aunts and uncles who I only met in later life. As a child these were the ones who participated in nurturing and encouraging us. Many have since passed on but their memories are precious and their views and beliefs very much a part of my identity.

I attended Cowper Street Primary School from the age of five to eleven years. I have a childhood memory of walking home from primary school holding hands with a little girl in my class. I don't remember her name, but I remember I wanted to go to her house to play so I had to go home first and get my mother's permission. This child left school a few years later to go and live on a farm in Yorkshire. I always wonder what happened to her. I also vividly recall walking home from primary school with a relative and playing blind man's bluff. I led her safely and carefully when it was my turn; but when it was her turn, she led me straight into a lamp-post. This was to prove significant in later life, as she led me into several lamp-posts, metaphorically speaking, as we got older. In fact it might be argued that the term lamp-post became a symbol for the deceitful and manipulative things which occurred.

After primary school I attended Scotthall Secondary Modern School, in Leeds. I have fond memories of the teachers and the many friends who also attended the school. It was at this school that I developed a passion for lawn tennis, primarily because the gym teacher was very keen on the sport, and encouraged her classes during wimbledon to sit in the hall and watch the tournament. To this day I really enjoy the sport, and although I do not play I am a fan of many of the greats such as Arthur Ashe, John McEnroe and more recently the William sisters. Although there was some attempt to teach us french, I never quite mastered it, but have always wanted to learn another language so recently took up spanish.

My wish to acquire another language stems from my father who would speak to us in a papiamento, a broken spanish. "Do it properly" he would say, "Poco Lia" as he showed me how to develop good penmanship or helped with some aspect of my homework. I have very fond memories of my father who I believe was an honourable man. He was a loving man and a good father.

My father worked in a factory in Leeds. As a first generation immigrant he was not afforded all the opportunities that his education could have bestowed. His priorities with regards to money were not as they should have been either, as he should have brought his wage packet home and not spent it gambling. Nevertheless he made it up to my siblings and I in other ways. One specific memory I have is that he would ensure all of his children, who were eligible, attended his works outing. His employers held a christmas party for the children of their employees every year and I remember going to several pantomimes and having a great feast afterwards. All the children were then given presents before departing for home.

Dad was a man of few words, but a loving and affectionate man. I remember as a teenager putting make up on him when he fell asleep in the chair and painting his finger nails with a bright coloured nail polish; all to great amusement when he awoke and looked in the mirror. I was very proud to go shopping with him, and vividly remember him buying me my first hot pants suit. In addition he always bought beautiful and thoughtful birthday cards, some of which I have kept to this day.

One day when I was about seventeen years old my father came into my room and said something to me, but I couldn't understand a word he was saying. "What's that Dad?" I asked. He repeated it, and it sounded like gobble dee gook. Later I learned he was trying to say something to the effect that he had gone to the bank, but 'I can't seem to get my words right.' At first my sister and I thought it was funny, but then realised something was wrong and phoned my mother at work.

When my mother came home my father was taken to hospital. He had suffered his first stroke. Over the years he was to suffer a great deal of frustration, because he was an intelligent man, and it must have been difficult not being able to express himself in his usual articulate way. He was very stoical about it however, and despite his physical disability returned to work a few months later. As a matter of interest I believe that one of my sisters' and I look like our Dad. We both have the same shaped lips, noses and protruding eyes. My father also told me as I was growing up that I resembled his youngest sister; and over the years as we corresponded and she sent pictures this seemed to be the case. However it was only when I met her in Jamaica while on vacation some years ago, that I fully comprehended how much we 'favour' one another. My father will always be remembered with a lot of love and some sadness.

My parents were not too religious, however they both believed in God, and as children we were sent to sunday school on a regular basis. We were taught the bible and took part in church events, this included going to Skegness as part of a church outing. Later when we became teenagers we attended the local church youth club. I was a fun loving teenager, with many friends both girls and boys and we socialized at the local clubs and often went to 'Blues'.(Blues for those of you who are not in the know is a party where you pay for your drinks, and sometimes for entry into the party). It was the time of Jim Reeves, of reggae music with artists such as Desmond Decker, bell bottom trousers, skinny rib tops and platform shoes.

Growing up in Leeds during the seventies was exciting and interesting. It was a period when black culture was shaping itself taking much of its ideas from North America, but also developing its own. I recall going to see a popular film at the time which starred Jimmy Cliff and was entitled '*The Harder They Come,*' which reinforced my identity as a black person. There were few black role models in the media, and very few television programmes with black actors. It was a time when Mohammed Ali, then Cassius Clay was considered too forthright, and proud. He was particularly famous for predicting which round he would beat his opponent in. He was for many a role model, a high profile sportsman who was in touch with his identity, and who was the heavy weight boxer of the world.

Like tennis, boxing is one of my favourite sports. I recall as a young girl the whole family would congregate around the black and white television to watch Cassius Clay's boxing matches, each making their own commentary over the official commentator as the fight progressed. 'Hit him, what happen you never know you should duck" and "leave the man's pretty face alone". These and similar other encouraging remarks often accompanied the fights.

We lived quite close to Potternewton Park in Leeds which borders Harehills and Chapeltown. Many of the dances and parties which we attended were in Chapeltown, although we also went to dances in other towns such as Huddersfield. Around 1974/1975 there began a series of attacks on prostitutes, in and around North Yorkshire. The reign of terror by Peter Sutcliffe, also known as the Yorkshire Ripper had begun. I mention it because as a young woman coming home in the early morning from a party or blues, occasionally on my own, it was a dangerous thing to do. I was living in dangerous times, because If I had been mistaken for a prostitute, I believe he made several mistakes when choosing his victims, there was a possibility of being attacked.

Peter Sutcliffe murdered thirteen women and attempted to kill others in his reign of terror in North Yorkshire, England. He is said to have sent tapes and letters to the police going so far as to sign them Jack the Ripper. The analogy between his crimes and that of the ripper in Victorian Society were essentially very similar. He used a hammer to knock his victims out and then used instruments of torture on them. Like the original ripper he committed the most gruesome acts on those who he maimed and killed. He was finally caught some ten years later and institutionalized at Broadmoor, a high-security psychiatric hospital in Berkshire, England. [2]

I left school at the age of fifteen, which was the norm in the early seventies. There was a possibility of staying on to take either CSE's or GCE's depending on which school you attended, but most of the immigrant children in my school year were encouraged to leave the school and find work in a factory. I was fortunate as my parent were keen for me to continue my education even if I did not stay on at school to take my GCE's. I was given several choices and opted to take a secretarial course and study for my GCE 'O' and GCE 'A' levels at the same time. I was quite successful in this chosen course and at eighteen years of age went to work for Barclays Bank.

I finally left home and moved to London when I was twenty one years of age and began working for the National Westminster Bank. This was an interesting period in my life, a time when I explored the bright lights of London, in addition to learning how to fend for myself. I met my mother's step-brother and his family who were supportive of me if life became particularly difficult; such as one landlord throwing acid over all of my clothes. There were also moments in my life when I experienced loneliness living in a bedsit; but fortunately I met some really wonderful people in one of the houses where I finally lived before getting my own flat. The other occupants of the house and I became friends as well as housemates and socialized in the home as well as going out together as a group. I rang home often and also visited Leeds on many occasions returning to my favourite meal specially prepared by my mother of bakes, mackerel and scramble cabbage. Finally when I felt more settled in London, I left the bank and returned to full time study. I began a university course in 1981 studying for a degree in english and subsequently a PGCE. Thereafter whilst working in full-time education, I studied and received a master's degree in cultural studies in 1995.

In my first teaching post I was a course tutor to young people who were disaffected with the traditional curriculum, and who were essentially disinterested in education. The schooling system of the mid 80s had failed them, and it was for post 16 educators to try to re-engage them in the educational process. To some extent I felt an empathy with these young people, as some of their experiences could be juxtaposed with my own.

As an educator I was encouraged to teach about topical subject areas to encourage the learner to participate in the learning process and make it more relevant to their lives. The topic of HIV and AIDS was very topical during this time and as part of my role I encouraged these young people to take responsibility for their sexual health. There were many rumours and much speculation about the origin of the disease. One is that it originated in Africa and another that it was created as a weapon. In today's society the disease is more or less under control and there seems less prejudice against those who are infected. I have retained an affection for my first students, and often wonder where they are and how they fared after leaving college.

During the mid-eighties I worked in a full time capacity as a lecturer up until the mid-nineties when I changed to becoming a part-time lecturer. I also became involved in other activities such as running an educational charity. I enjoyed teaching english literature, although at times my experiences were similar to the hero of the novel *Wilt* by Tom Sharpe. It was sometimes difficult to motivate disinterested students who were simply re-taking their GCSE's because they needed the subject to take the course in which they were really interested.

> "In the novel *Wilt*, the eponymous hero of the novel, Henry Wilt is a demoralized and professionally under-rated assistant lecturer who teaches literature to uninterested construction apprentices at a community college in the south of England. It is his exploits and assessment of his students and his own life which provides the hilarious comedy which is expressed throughout the novel." [3]

I enjoyed working with the students, and while ploughing through *Macbeth* at times proved difficult I felt a great sense of satisfaction when the students achieved the required grades.

As well as part-time teaching in english and business studies, I ran an educational charity which was founded and developed in order to raise the achievement and educational potential of young people in the local area. It was time consuming and hard work and involved gaining funding to ensure its continuance. We were fairly fortunate in getting funds from the national lottery. Although there was a committee it really was a one woman show. Two of my sisters and a cousin (who took over as chairperson when I resigned) had initially been supportive, but had other time constraints. My role as a director and founder of the charity was interesting and diverse, and I excelled in this particular field. I suppose like my late uncle I am something of a human rights campaigner, and the charity allowed me to support disadvantaged children. In addition we ran a summer and saturday school to encourage academic excellence for all young people.

The year 1990 began with fresh hope as we witnessed Nelson Mandela, anti-apartheid activist, who had been imprisoned for 27 years being released from prison in February of that year. Nelson Mandela later became president of South Africa a wise and humble man who for me was an inspiration and a role model. There were many significant and personal events which took place during this decade including the then president of America, Bill Clinton almost being impeached for lying about a scandal in which he was involved. It was also when I learned that a relative had published a short story which damaged my father's reputation.

The nineties presented numerous difficulties, and the profound loss of my mother who passed away in 1993. My mother is and always will be the most precious person in my life. She was my friend, at times my confidante and the most important influence in my life. I often visited Canada when my mother emigrated to live with my sisters in the late eighties. We spoke regularly on the phone and also corresponded by letter. Her beautiful personality would shine through with the golden dress which she sometimes wore, which not only suited her personality but her inner radiance. It is she who made me believe in myself and encouraged me when at times things seemed insurmountable. "Don't give up she would say for if you give up now success may just be around the corner." I have learned to be a very determined person, knowing that whatever the obstacle perseverance is ultimately the key to success.

My mother often spoke to me about quitting smoking. Neither of my parents drank or smoked, in fact my father often asked, when he realised that I had adopted the habit, "why I was practising to smoke?" I know they would both be very proud that I have finally given up that nasty habit and I am now smoke free. I have never drunk strong alcohol but would sometimes drink wine and champagne. I found however, the drinking of wine produced a negative reaction so gave up drinking altogether some twenty years ago.

I bought my first house in April of the same year as I lost my mother. I am still sad that she has never had the opportunity of visiting me in my then new home. It was a three bedroom semi-detached in a suburban area in London, England. It was in this new home in August 1997 that I heard of the tragic passing of the Princess of Wales. We had just completed our first ever summer school, and felt a tremendous sense of achievement that the children had shown great improvement in their grades in addition to providing a concert which was well received.

I was in the process of decorating the living room and listening to the radio at the same time, when suddenly an announcement was made over the radio that Princess Diana had been involved in a car crash in Paris, France. There was a great deal of uncertainty as to how serious the crash was, however it was believed that at least one person had died. As time went on it became increasingly evident from the reports that the crash was very serious indeed as there was talk of a few fatalities. Eventually it was announced that despite the hospital staff doing all they could that she had died. The outpouring of grief which followed from all was touching and very moving. I do not think there was a single person in the world who was not devastated by the loss of Princess Diana. I was especially moved when I saw the then young Prince Harry carrying a wreath entitled 'Mummy'. It brought back memories of my own mother who had died a few years before and I felt devastated by my loss and theirs.

I brought in the millennium with friends. The turn of a century, the year 2000, would I hope bring good things unfortunately it proved to be a very challenging period in my life. In 2001 I resigned as chairperson of the educational charity in need of a good rest. I gained it in spite of myself and in July ended up resting for two weeks in hospital. I entered the mental health system in July 2001, menopausal, burned out and drugged. I recovered and tried to move on. This was to prove difficult as there were many who took this opportunity to misuse, control and mishandle me during this period in my life.

I was trying to rest but finding it difficult, there were so many interruptions; and the things that were being said to me were very distressing. Day and night, no let up, just a constant stream of information. George the name was repeated like a refrain throughout, George, what was it about George? George was an ex-lover, who I had previously been friends with. The friendship had ended badly amidst speculation that he 'fancied' one of my relatives. At least that was the impression that he gave me. My neighbours were giving me another impression, that they'd had sex together. Could it be true, I was beside myself. It was years later in fact George and I had stopped speaking to each other since 1998, and it was now some three years later. It seemed out of place that I was being reminded of a relationship that was no longer in existence. Whoever was around the place whispering was giving too much information. After four days and nights without sleep I finally gave in and went to my sister's flat. I couldn't sleep despite the herbal medication I had taken.

In the morning having not slept, my sister suggested we go to the hospital. A friend of the family was staying at the house, but his presence was more of a distraction than a help. At the hospital my sister insisted that I tell the doctor that I was hearing voices. Stupidly I agreed although I insisted that it wasn't out of the norm. I have problems with my hearing, especially hearing background sounds. However, the doctor was concerned, suspecting some kind of paranoia and asked if I would stay in hospital on a voluntary basis. In hindsight I realised I should have declined and insisted on being given a much needed sleeping tablet and be sent home to get some sleep. However, that's now, after the event, I was too tired at the time to be particularly assertive. Unfortunately, I didn't take that course of action and was instead admitted to hospital, where I still found it difficult to sleep.

Finally, I decided I just wanted to go home, and was told that if I wanted to be released would have to sign a release form. I refused, as I had entered voluntarily and had not signed to come in, did not see why I should sign to come out. The doctor took exception and I was sectioned under the Mental Health Act for refusal to sign a release form. This is the most frightening thing that has ever happened to me. The consequences of being sectioned and restrained in a hospital can have far reaching consequences. It meant that my freedom was being denied, and I was now considered as a threat, in this instance to myself. I was restrained and given an injection which put me to sleep. I slept for twenty-four hours, after which I carried on as normal except that I was discouraged from hearing voices, a perfectly natural occurrence.

The doctors initially thought that I might be delusional, or translated, needed a good night's sleep. They later diagnosed anxiety and referred me to a psychologist. Neither diagnosis is accurate; I needed a good night's sleep without disturbance. I have often overheard the neighbours joking about my so called mental illness, responding when asked what was the matter with her that she was 'tired'. Many of the patients in the ward at the time also teased me by discussing Jesus Christ, and I remember whilst in a haze (induced by the injection I was given to help me to sleep) dreaming about our saviour.

I was kept in hospital for two weeks, after which I was referred to a psychologist. Prior to starting these sessions I was in the living room watching television when my attention was drawn to the news reader's shock at what was currently unfolding. At first they were unsure if the plane had accidently crashed hitting the building, but it soon became very obvious as the second plane crashed, and reports began coming in from other parts of America, that this was a deliberate act of war. America was attacked on September 11th 2001 by terrorists who crashed two planes into the twin towers of the World Trade Centre in New York. Another two planes which were hijacked and heading for Washington DC failed in their mission. The loss of lives and devastation shook the whole world, and it is said that nearly 3000 people died. Osama Bin Laden, an Islamic terrorist claimed responsibility. In May

2011 after many years at large Bin Laden was found and killed.[4]

I started sessions with a psychologist in January 2002, and had something like eight sessions which lasted over a few months. I believe he said something to the effect that capable people often forget to take care of themselves first. This is a view that my own mother lived by, that it is important that you care for yourself in addition to caring for others. I remember that I was decorating the kitchen at the time and the psychologist referred to this particular task as a means of demonstrating the psychology of caring for oneself.

Overall the sessions were useful, but I will always remember that I was led to believe that these people now had power over me, and could detain me at any time. There was the very real threat that I could be institutionalised for the rest of my life. I once questioned during a session with the psychologist something which seemed to be occurring outside the door, "what's that?" I queried. His response was "nothing". Nothing turned out to be sounds, other people's voices and regular sounds, i.e. traffic, the wind, the rain and so on . . . "That's nothing".

In the intervening years, I came to understand that some people need to control others, and remain in charge. They need to have power over another human being, and in entering the mental health system I became vulnerable to those who needed to be in control. I personally believe that I should never have been threatened, and it causes me concern as to how people within the mental health system are treated and regarded, by mental health practitioners as well as the general public as a whole.

I am mentally well and emotionally healthy, and I believe this can be attributed, to the fact that there was nothing mentally or emotionally wrong with me, and two my faith in God. It is after my experience in the hospital, that I realised that I needed to give my life totally to Christ, and I became a born again christian in 2001 and was fully baptised in 2003.

My experience in the psychiatric wing of the hospital brought to mind several literary associations. I thought of the novel *Jane Eyre*, by Charlotte Bronte which discusses the mad wife in the attic, as well as a more general love story about a governess who fell in love with her employer. The mad wife, whose illness it is suggested was inherited is alienated from her husband, who all but wishes her dead. It seems the feeling is mutual as she sets fire to his bed in the middle of the night when she escapes one night from the attic. The idea of someone else taking control of your life, and locking you up, is quite frightening. She is presented as a dangerous lunatic who is inarticulate and seems to communicate ineffectively. Rochester, the central hero of the novel in discussing his insane wife says in Chapter 26 to Jane Eyre:

"Bertha Mason is mad and she came of a mad family; idiots and maniacs through three generations".[5]

Another literary association is the poem *'Mental Cases'* by Wilfred Owen who was a World War I soldier and poet. He was one of the first poet's to discuss neuralgia or post-traumatic stress disorder. In the poem he vividly describes those soldiers for whom war was too much, and their minds are no longer their own. Instead they live in imagined worlds, reliving the experience and horrors of war. Essentially these men have gone insane because of the horrors which they have seen and experienced during the war. As the poet Wilfred Owen states, his job is to warn of the horror of war and the pity war instils.

> "Who are these-Why sit they here in twilight? These are men whose minds the Dead have ravished . . . Multitudinous murders they once witnessed" [6]

People vary in their attitudes to mental illness in today's society, and for the most part I have found that some can be insensitive to other people's feelings. One way of disguising any uncertainty they may feel is to laugh or mock this particular sickness. My own experience within the mental health system has engendered and even encouraged a more sympathetic approach to those with a mental illness. I believe that mental illness or any kind of illness is not something we would wish for ourselves or for another. If we are fortunate enough never to have the experience then we should be thankful. I have met many people over the years, whether it is in my professional or social life who have a mental illness and it doesn't make them stupid or less than a person, it means they are living with an illness which makes life more difficult for them.

Given my experience I am far more conscious about ensuring that physically and mentally I am functioning as I should, this means getting the required hours of sleep. At one time the medication I was taking for my blood pressure was slowing me down too much. For some reason 'care in the community' or 'psychological experiment' encouraged the taking of prescription drugs which slowed me down to the extent that I sometimes fell asleep in the street. This left me exposed, literally in some instances to interference and abuse.

In early 2006 after a visit to Canada to visit my sisters I came back to England alert, confident and able to once again reclaim my independence. What I am going to relay is going to shock an audience, and I swear it is true. I didn't know, but apparently it was common knowledge that a key to my house had been found. Or at least that is what was claimed. It had apparently been lost in the street. I awoke one night, I had not locked the bedroom door, and there was a man standing in the room, a candle in his hand. He was standing about eight feet away, just watching me. I was terrified, and realised I had to keep totally still. He knew he had woken me though and said:

"I'm not going to hurt you, go back to sleep". My subconscious must have recognised the voice and trusted the person because I did go back to sleep. Thereafter I ensured the bedroom door was locked. This and other instances make me realise how vulnerable I was to either rape, abuse, or being murdered in the house where I lived. I later learned that the neighbours would enter my house; either by climbing in through the window or using the key which they had found and interfere with my food. I wasn't necessarily aware they were there, either because I was in another room and couldn't hear them, because they had entered the premises when I was out, or because it was late at night and I was asleep.

I was definitely drugged when I came back from Canada in 2006, although I didn't know then exactly what was wrong with me, just that I was not functioning as effectively as I had been two weeks previously when I arrived back in England. One night when I had been kept awake, I believe the neighbours were putting me back into some kind of routine; so I would no longer be independent able to think and make decisions for myself, I was aware of someone talking to me and making threats.

It was a man, and he was saying quite unpleasant things. I'm not certain if he was in the house or immediately outside, but I knew I was no longer safe. I waited until daylight and then left my bedroom so I could use the phone in the hallway. The person who was interfering with me was still making comments. I phoned for an ambulance, I needed someone to check what was going on. It was very early in the morning, but I knew if I did not call for help that this man was going to hurt me. When the ambulance arrived some ten minutes later

I could not find the key to let them in, someone had removed them. The police were in attendance with the ambulance but I could not let them in. There was the smell of sex in the dining room, as if someone had recently been intimate in the room. Many stories abound as to why this might be the case, none of them involve me being sexually active. In order to let the police and ambulance driver into the house I had to phone a friend who was a key holder. She arrived and when the police came in the premises were searched. If anyone had been in the house, they'd had a chance to escape.

To this day I don't know who it was, however one particular man was placed on a supervision order by the police with regards to his proximity to me. I am very fortunate and can only imagine the dangers I have been exposed to by people entering my home without my consent; interference with me on the street and abuse; whether it be physical or emotional, by those who took exception to something I may have repeated in my sleep.

It is my firm belief that I live under grace, because that's the only reason I could possibly have survived in such circumstances. It is truly a miracle that I have to date survived the banging on the walls, the screaming and shouting at me in the street and being drugged. Another reason why I have survived thus far is because of the 'unsung heroes' who came to my rescue. One such person to whom I owe a debt of gratitude is a police officer serving in the Metropolitan Police Force his name I believe is Sarge.

CHAPTER TWO

PSYCHOLOGICAL PHENOMENON

Friday 26th August 2011

Cruz Bay, St John, USVI

I have rented a self-catering apartment in Cruz Bay which overlooks the sea. It's for a short period of time, but I feel quite settled and able to continue writing my autobiography. The apartment is unusual in that it has two levels, the bedroom and bathroom on the top floor and the kitchen and living room on the ground floor. It reminds me of an apartment which I had in London, England which also had two levels, but there the similarity ends.

In 1995 it was brought to my attention that a distant cousin had written a book or should I call it a short story documenting briefly what life had been like for her when she lived with my parents in Leeds during the sixties and seventies. This published account of life at 11A Avenue Crescent Leeds 8, was discussed in what she referred to as flashbacks of her early childhood.[7] I am not a mental health practitioner, and my own experiences are not sufficient to give a personal account about flashbacks. I therefore referred to a computer website to get a definition.

In psychological terms a flashback is an involuntary recurrent memory or a psychological phenomenon in which an individual has a sudden usually powerful, re-experience of a past experience or elements of a past experience. The experience can be happy, sad, exciting or any other emotion. The term is used when the memory is re-called involuntarily, and/or when it is so intense that the person "relives" the experience, unable to recognise it as a memory, and not something that is happening in real time.[8]

Essentially she claims to have experienced a flashback of being abused by my father. I cannot completely refute this, and my father is no longer alive to defend his reputation, but what I can say is this. This distant cousin joined the family in the sixties when she came from St Kitts with my grandmother Ruth Ann Cranston. My grandmother suffered a stroke within the first months of living in England and died. It was a very sad time for all; we were just getting to know her and her loss was deeply felt. This cousin had been adopted by my grandmother who was a distant cousin of her grandfather. Both of her parents were dead but she had two siblings who were living.

Despite having six children of her own my mother decided to let this young lady remain with the family; as her grandfather was not interested nor any other of her closer living relatives in having her to live with them. My mother approached social services who provided some assistance and she effectively became a foster parent. She had been one for many years on an ad hoc basis for those who came to our home throughout the years. This was however on a more formal basis.

As closest in age to my cousin (I was about seven or eight years old and she was a year older) we shared a room in the attic next to my father. My mother and father did not always share a room for a variety of reasons. However, my memories of him are that of a loving and caring man, who was very much a gentleman.

My cousin was a bright and imaginative child who received pocket money from social services as well as a clothing and travel allowance. She was a clever child and passed her 11/13 plus. In those days it meant that she could attend the grammar school. She was certainly exposed to an elitist education as well as influences outside of the ones I had. She made friends with a few classmates and they all participated in making up love stories about their favourite pop idols. If memory serves the pop group the Monkees played a large part in these very sexually explicit love stories written by my cousin's classmates. I suppose this together with the love stories she read fuelled her imagination.

I remember this cousin being more sexually aware than most, she discussed having periods and made comments about some girl who smelled different, which she thought was because of her period. She was very interested in boys and when we went to the youth club she encouraged me to chat up boys. I was relatively shy and did not do as she suggested. My cousin ran home in shock one day claiming that some man was in the alley way exposing himself. The police were called, but the perpetrator had run away. She started dating quite early I believe at the age of thirteen she was allowed to go to the cinema with a young man whose mother was a friend of my mother.

Finally, she admitted her first sexual experience to me. I learned that at the age of approximately fifteen or sixteen years she lost her virginity with a young man, who it seems also broke her heart. On the basis of these things, and the fact that my father was not always at home, I think it very unlikely that the flashbacks relate to my late father. She never recounted having a sexual experience with him whilst living with us; nor has she whilst living at 11A Avenue Crescent, Leeds ever spoke to my mother, any of my siblings or myself about having been abused by my father. I take on board that her argument is perhaps that she had no recall at the time, but she certainly use to make very negative comments and bitch about all of the family. As I recall several people warned my mother to be careful of her because she was not grateful that she had somewhere to live and call home.

My cousin left 11A Avenue Crescent, Leeds 8, amidst controversy. My eldest sister can be something of a troublemaker, and she was involved in a confrontation with a man at a party. Several of us had attended the party, but I was the only one to go outside and see the fight in progress. Of course I joined in. Unfortunately both my sister and I got our 'arses' kicked. After the fight this particular relative was picked on for not joining in. In her defence she was inside the party like everyone else and unaware of what was happening; however, she felt wrongly accused and left the family home. She actually had been awarded a place at teacher training college and this was sent on to her. I don't know where she went when she left home, but she was sadly missed as we were close at the time. However time moves on and I am pleased to say that she succeeded at college and became a teacher.

After the death of both my parents and in the midst of grief I was made aware of this published story. I felt somewhat betrayed that my parents who had provided a home for this relative and had been very supportive of her, were disrespected and accused of abusing this poor orphan. I often wonder why when both of my parents were no longer able to refute the allegations she felt it was the most appropriate time to discuss her 'flashback'? In addition I wonder what her ingratitude was about? One suggestion is that she might have been jealous of a loving family; we were poor but happy.

Although we may not always have paid the electricity bill on time, and needed candles to see, this offered an opportunity for us as children to sit huddled close together playing word games and making up amusing stories.

Furthermore, if her short story is a true and accurate reflection of my father why did she wait for such a long period of time to make her views known? One school of thought is that the law says that you cannot slander the dead. This might imply that this cousin waited until she believed there was no one to refute her claim thus no libellous action could be taken against her. I certainly consulted a solicitor at the time with a view to suing her for defamation of my father's character. However this was to no avail as you" cannot slander the dead".[9]

In her brief discussion of life at 11A Avenue Crescent my cousin presents us with a discussion of all her mothers. She talks of her own mother who tragically died before she knew her. She discusses mama, who was actually my grandmother, Ruth Ann Cranston, who nurtured and loved her. Finally she remembers my mother, who through her formative and teenage years provided a foundation for her to grow and achieve academic success. I really wish that in writing she had presented a more accurate interpretation of the role of both my mother and father in supporting her during her early life.

I genuinely believe the truth will find its way some day. I leave you to decide for yourselves whether you think this honourable, noble and wonderful man would have done such a thing. No one else has ever made such a claim. I certainly was not abused by my father.

Though I am painfully aware of someone who was lovers with her own father (not mine). This person's tragic story is in stark contrast to my cousin's flashback. This is an actual memory about someone who ran in fear for her life. It calls into question man's ability to commit horrible, vile acts on a child. It opens a whole debate on the role of children who are essentially the responsibility of adult society and should be cared and loved instead of being sexually and/or emotionally abused. Interestingly in African Society it is the whole village that raises a child, each adult ensuring that they promote a healthy self-esteem, and the physical welfare of the child.

The abuse of children is well documented in a variety of sources, not least of which are sociological and psychological journals. It is also the subject of literature and some talk shows. In the 1982 novel and film *The Color Purple* by Alice Walker, the central protagonist delineates her struggle in a male alienated world. It is a world where the only person she has to talk to is God, and as her step-father repeatedly rapes her, and she produces two children, she writes letters to God. A moving and poignant story of abuse in a southern state in America. The narrative also illustrates the role of black females during the 1930s in the Southern Unites States.

> "Celie, the protagonist and narrator of the novel The Color Purple is a poor, uneducated, fourteen year old black girl living in rural Georgia. Celie starts to write letters to God because her stepfather Alphonso, beats and rapes her . . . The title of the novel The Color Purple is continually equated with suffering and pain."[10]

This literary piece can be compared and contrasted with Maya Angelou's book '*I know Why the Caged Bird Sings*' which gives a striking account of a young girl growing up in the south of America amidst Jim Crow laws. The novel, *I Know Why the Caged Bird Sings* is the 1969 autobiographical novel about the early years of African American writer and poet Maya Angelou. The book covers topics common to autobiographies written by black american women in the years following the civil rights movement. A celebration of motherhood, a critique of racism, the importance of family and the quest for independence, personal dignity and self-definition.[11]

Angelou uses her autobiography to explore subjects such as identity, rape, racism and literacy . . . She also assesses a black woman's life in a male dominated society. At the age of eight years old Maya Angelou was raped. This compares with the life of the central protagonist, Celie in *The Color Purple*, and it may be argued that as women of color they shared similar experiences. Although one difference is that the novel *The Color Purple* is a fictional autobiography whilst *I Know Why The Caged Bird Sings* is a factual account of the author's life. I have attempted to discuss some of these themes in my autobiography; as I am also a black woman writing my life story within the confines of a male dominated society. In addition it was important to assess the importance of family in my life, to discuss my need for independence and to try desperately to hold onto my personal dignity.

In addition to these themes the subject of abuse is one which I have addressed in several contexts; initially from a general point of view through to a more subjective assessment. In discussing my own personal circumstances I found it useful to provide a definition, and consider my situation in the light of the definition. The definition of abuse is said to to be actions which cause physical injury, leaves marks and causes pain. It may involve biting, choking, burning, pinching, biting, hitting, kicking, punching or throwing things at the person. It may also involve calling the person names and accusing them of wrong doing (not necessarily criminal).

Abuse can also be sexual, emotional, verbal or a combination of all. Abuse can also be neglect essentially not taking care of someone's basic needs. This is particularly applicable to children, the elderly or someone who is incapacitated in some way. Sexual abuse is classified as any type of sexual contact between an adult and anyone younger than 18 years of age. If a family member sexually abuses another family member this is called incest. Emotional abuse can be the most difficult to identify, because there are no outward signs of the abuse.

Emotional abuse may involve yelling, screaming, threatening and constantly criticising the person. It can be very damaging to the recipient's self-esteem and feelings of self-worth. Interestingly enough abuse can also take the form of hate crimes directed at people because of their race, religion, abilities, gender, or sexual orientation. Recognising abuse may be especially difficult for someone who has lived with it for years. The abused person may actually think it's the norm, especially if they have been in an abusive situation for years.

The possibility of the abused person blaming themselves has also been well documented, and often they are lead to believe it's their fault. It's very important to note that abuse is never the fault of the person being abused. Sometimes abusers manipulate those they are abusing by telling them they did something wrong or asked for it in some way.

This is not true, the abuser and not the abused is at fault. [12] For instance, I have been made aware that I repeat information in my sleep. I have always 'talked' in my sleep, but over the years neighbours, friends and family began to question me in my sleep, and encouraged me to repeat information, which did not necessarily conform to my own thoughts or views. I was perceived as 'dotish', because of this interference in my life.

I was encouraged to repeat comments in my sleep which were derogatory and inappropriate. These remarks were often about other people, many of whom were neither friends nor acquaintances of mine, but of the person who wished me to repeat the comment. As far as I am concerned interfering with someone who falls asleep or is asleep is abuse. It is in no way my fault that you may rationalise the reason for physically abusing me, by stating that I repeated an inappropriate remark, which hurt your feelings when the original comment is not mine. Whosoever, encouraged this over the years, and perpetrated it is very guilty of abuse. There is no justification for treating anyone in this way.

Sometime ago I was led to believe that I had made some filthy, disgusting remarks about my own mother. I have no memory of this but the comments have been repeated while I was awake, and the remarks are indeed filthy. Again, I would reiterate that I am the one being abused. I have no wish to make filthy comments in my sleep, especially against my own mother. It is interference of the worst kind, and should never take place, nor should it continue.

This particular piece of information has been highlighted and is being perpetuated wherever I go. It seems one particular relative is very keen to ensure that the comments 'stick' to me, despite the fact that they were actually said by someone else, and put for me to repeat in my sleep. The disgusting comments are repeated, either through previously recorded comments, or by someone repeating it, and it is then discussed in a quite common place manner, as if it should be a subject in the public arena. I dispute this quite strongly, as the comments are private, and I have never given anyone permission to use me in this way. I am very concerned that at the time of writing these comments are still being made, and now believe will have to take legal action to stop the on-going disgusting remarks being made.

I was very much a 'mummy's girl and it is totally horrendous to me that I have disrespected my mother in this way. Not only have I disrespected my mother, but the comments were repeated for years, as an excuse for abusing me. I refer to physical as well as emotional abuse; hitting and screaming and shouting at me. It seems that all and sundry believed it was justification for abusing, shunning, treating me as a leper and basically making life as difficult as they possibly could. This includes overcharging and ripping me off.

One wonders how these things began. Well, it seems that one of my relative's would stand outside of the front door and say disgusting things to me. It was evident to her that I could not hear everything which she said, so instead of letting me know that I was only hearing partially, she chose to abuse me instead. She would then come into the house and behave as if nothing was amiss.

A friend of mine who was staying with me at the time was outraged and could not believe the behaviour she was exhibiting and the inappropriate communication that was being made. I am aware of some of these things because in some instances what she has said has been repeated by others, and I have also heard some of her inappropriate remarks and comments.

In time the neighbours started to repeat the things that family members and friends began saying often going so far as to tape the comments. Hence the four nights and days that I could not sleep was because I was being wised up. It was too much information over too short a period of time, the intent was perhaps positive, but everyone needs to sleep and absorb information.

In time it became the norm to repeat things which other people with a grievance or grudge came along and said. Put that for her to repeat in her sleep. One particular ex-boyfriend's partner who I believe was said to be looking after me, would come along in the day when the children were coming home from school and say the filthiest four letter words. However instead of the parents objecting they would say something to the effect of 'put it for the crazy lady to say in her sleep'. My sleep pattern was interrupted for years, and as I slept less and less I became a shadow of my former self, with dark circles under my eyes like a panda bear. I often fell asleep in the street, dribbled so all could hear my every thought and my life was no longer my own as I was required to repeat other people's comments whilst asleep.

It then became the norm for people who I had no relationship with to say put that for her to say in her sleep, or tell her to confess to a particular indiscretions and say that she is the perpetrator. I have even been led to believe that the police used me to investigate a crime. If you have any knowledge of what took place either call crime stoppers or ask Miss Cuffy to repeat the comments in her sleep. One particular neighbour started a business, which entailed him working for customers who wanted him to abuse me or put comments for me to repeat while asleep.

Another more physical form of abuse is fingering a person's genitalia without permission and participating in oral sex with someone who is technically asleep. This is abuse of the worst kind, as it would involve taking advantage of someone, and essentially making them a victim of sexual abuse akin to rape. Would this make the victim a slut? I think not, it places that person in a position to take some kind of legal action.

Surely it would be considered criminal for this to be taking place? Unzipping a person's clothing and touching their private parts is definitely sexual abuse. Unfortunately I have had the experience of someone touching my private part, and I reported it to the police. The matter was taken quite seriously and handled sensitively.

Any sexual abuse is wrong irrespective of what form it takes. Its effect on the person being abused can be detrimental and affect their life chances in many ways. I personally believe that if you internalize the abuse as being your fault in some way then the abuser wins. I once belonged to the co-counselling community in London, England which believes that all hurts and negativity in your life should be contradicted. It's important that you validate yourself and recognise that you are not at fault and certainly not to blame.

My contradiction in situations such as this is that I will not take in other people's negativity. I have a healthy self-esteem, am humble, healthy and stable. I love myself. I love that I am kind, honest, have lots of integrity and am a decent human being. I love that I am not dependent on others for my livelihood, and am financially independent. I love that I can just walk away without looking back. I am a strong black woman, able to make friends wherever I go.

I take on board that sometimes other people will not respond positively towards me, despite the fact that I am a good human being. Whenever this is the case I will not question it, but will dig even deeper to change my own negative response to that person. I also realise that at times we have to wait for a good response. I understand that it's best to be patient and hope for better things in my life. I know that I wish good for other people, and am very proud of that quality.

I should only ever expect good things and have had the best and now expect better to come. I have no wish to focus on negativity; I also have no wish to win or to lose, life is not a game with winners and losers. I will love me to the best of my ability and want good things for myself. I will endeavour to do the best for others and do not have overly high expectations. I believe co-counselling has been helpful, and has encouraged me to maintain a healthy approach in life. My faith in Christ has also ensured that there are no voids in my life, and I have achieved self-fulfilment despite the abuses experienced to date.

CHAPTER THREE

MAESTRO

Cruz Bay, St John, USVI

I am still in the same apartment that I mentioned yesterday, 26th August 2011. The exterior of the apartment has a small pool, and is quite high up on a hill overlooking the ocean. The sea is quite calm after the tropical storm which descended a few days ago. In contrast to the howling winds I can now hear a refreshing breeze blowing and whistling through the trees. There are banana trees, palm and coconut trees all around. In addition there are shrubs, some of which are giving off a beautiful scent. There are houses in clusters in the foreground. Many of the buildings are 2/3 storeys high and look like apartment buildings rather than lone houses. Some are light blue with beige and green tiles on the roof; others are beige with red tiles on the roof. The apartments and houses seem to ascend the hills almost like steps. There isn't much traffic just a few lorries on the road in the valley below. The occasional car that I see is heading for the ferry on its way home to St Thomas. There are two boats in the harbour, and one soon pulls out, its destination unknown. In the distances are from West to East a series of islands. Some inhabited, others only occupied by the birds and plant life which array the islands. There are 62 islands in this part of the world, and St Thomas can clearly be seen in the distance. It seems to be littered with houses, and in the evening the lights from the island make it look like a busy city. There are birds twittering in the background and a palm tree sways in the faint rustling breeze. The blue skies with billowy clouds make an attractive setting, and at this time of the day the sun is setting and casting a silvery glimmer over the sea. The island is not picturesque and is marred by unsightly cranes. This evening however it seems tranquil, as the motor boats skim aimlessly across the Caribbean Sea.

I met my first serious boyfriend when I was just 15 years old and visiting relatives in Birmingham. He was a gangly teenager, but proved to be my lifetime love. Although it's not reciprocated this man has affected and influenced my life in many ways. Maestro, at least that's what I called him, was for me something of a seer. As you go through life you meet people, some who make an impression on you, and others who influence and affect your life in ways you could not even imagine. Maestro, was the latter, he was someone who I had a great deal of respect for and looked up to as someone who was knowledgeable and intelligent.

We met when two of my cousins invited me to go to Birmingham with them. It was fun travelling on the coach and I recall one of my cousin's making jokes about the cows resembling certain relatives. We attended a dance and we also visited a place called The Organisation. It was the early seventies, a time when young black people were very 'black conscious,' and recognised the need to stand up and be pro-active. Horrendous race crimes were taking place; and many black people, especially Asians were the victims of physical violence at the hands of the then National Front. The American Civil Rights was very prominent and famous people such as Malcolm X and Angela Davis were at the forefront of politics.

The late 1960s and early 1970s was a time of significant progress and political activity in its fight against racism. There were demonstrations by the African Caribbean community against yet more anti-immigration laws. There was also an increasing number of protest campaigns against the National Front, police harassment and racist educational policies. It was in this climate of exposing racism and racist's propaganda that for the first time large numbers of black and white people, concentrated in unity to combat racism. Two huge carnivals were launched, Notting Hill Gate in London and one in Leeds, Yorkshire to encourage and foster feelings of goodwill within the community. [13]

I remember at this time a good friend of my mother who was an active community educator and also a headteacher of a primary school, encouraged myself and a group of other young people to attend a radio broadcast to give our views, as young black people. We also visited a police station to discuss our concerns about police harassment. There was a great deal of concern about anti-immigration laws at the time, and I vividly remember joining in a march where we advocated that we should 'take the pass and wipe a certain part of our anatomy.'

Young black people became black conscious and joined in the struggle with black political activists in America. The American Civil Rights Movement was very prominent and people such as Martin Luther King, Eldridge Cleaver, Angela Davis and Malcolm X became causes in the struggle against racism and in the fight against injustice. In this political climate, The Organisation had a house where black activists held meetings. There were also the beginnings of saturday schools which raised cultural awareness, as well as ensured basic literacy and numeracy skills were available to its children. The aims and objectives of this community led group was to raise black consciousness as well as support those in the community who needed it. This could be the elderly, those who were seeking legal as well as moral support, or others who had been victims of police brutality.

It was in this environment that I met Maestro, a tall gangly cheeky young man, seventeen years of age. I was to love this man for two decades before he vanished from my life for almost twenty years. We were young and he lived in Birmingham while I lived in Leeds. I had other boyfriends and he had other girlfriends. In fact he had two children at a young age while living in Birmingham. However, he had made a distinct impression on me, and he would telephone me in Leeds and I would telephone him in Birmingham.

A few years later one of my sisters' moved to Birmingham to train as a nurse, and I would visit her on occasions. Her then boyfriend, who is now her husband of some forty plus years was an acquaintance of Maestro, and we often frequented the same clubs and dances. On these occasions as the DJ played Marvin Gaye, *What's Going On* or a Curtis Mayfield track Maestro would stand aloof, and I would longingly look at him wishing he would ask me to dance. This was often to no avail, as he was smitten by some other female in the club. Eventually, we started dating, and as time went on we became serious. At the age of seventeen we started courting properly. He visited my parents in Leeds and I visited his family in Birmingham.

He proposed marriage when I was eighteen years old and I accepted. However when he moved to Leeds he was unfaithful, and broke my heart. You would think that decades later I would have learned my lesson, but no I still trusted and believed this man was honourable and would not lie to me. Our relationship ended when I discovered that he was seeing other women, and after my twenty first birthday, I moved from Leeds to live in London.

I met and fell in love again at the age of twenty three years, and eventually lived with Navaro until I was thirty years or so years of age. You would think that once he knew I was settled in another relationship that Maestro, would simply move on.

This however, did not seem to stop him from visiting, and even on occasions from staying with us. Navaro was a very understanding man.

During my relationship with this particular partner who was very encouraging I went back to study and took a degree at university. I then entered teacher training college. Unfortunately this relationship broke down because of my inability to have children. I have a condition known as endometriosis, and whilst I could perhaps have conceived through artificial insemination by donor, the strain on the relationship was too much and this particular option was never fully explored. Somethings are not meant to be, and I am pleased that Navaro married and had several children.

A year or so after the break up with Navaro I received an unexpected telephone call from Maestro. He was back in the country, he had moved to Jamaica several years before; and he wanted to visit me. I was very excited by this and we even went to a party which was held by my cousin that evening. We became lovers a few months later, and over the years he came and went, spending time in Jamaica and time in England. There was no pressure for him to commit, essentially he's the type of man, I learned from experience that needs to be free. There are times when he just likes to be alone, not necessarily because he was being unfaithful, but he just needed to be on his own.

We came to an informal understanding and he was very supportive when, in trying to have a baby, it became evident that I could not conceive. He was reassuring and said it was unimportant he didn't want any more children. This man was someone who I valued and who was very important to me. I thought of him as a friend and confidante, as well as lover. We grew up together as teenagers, shared a Christmas as a family with my parents in Leeds, and it seemed cared for each other. Maestro was a person whom I would have trusted with my life.

When I moved in 1989 to a smaller flat, he was the one who offered the additional financial support that was needed to buy the property. I believe at this stage he was happy and we had established a stable relationship, based on trust and mutual respect. One of my sister's was living with me at the time, and she stayed in the old flat, whilst I moved into the new one. Maestro went back to Jamaica, but within a few months was back in England. I was surprised, could it be that he had missed me?

He moved in with me and for a very short time I was happy. That is until we went to a party with a group of his and my sister's friends. That night, despite the fact that we were living together as a couple, he totally ignored me, and spent the night flirting and dancing with my sister's friend, who he had met for the first time, and it appears fancied. Memories of the times when I had been ignored in Birmingham re-surfaced, and to avoid showing how embarrassed and hurt I was by his behaviour I went outside and sat in the car until everyone was ready to leave. I suppose if I act like a doormat, then I am treated as a doormat. He often mockingly called me a martyr. A few days later when he wanted affection from me I was unable to respond, and we ended up having a huge row. I told him never to come back, and he never has; that really was the end of our relationship.

I saw him a few years later at Leeds carnival sitting in the park holding his latest child, a mixed race little boy. I walked straight past him, unable to think of a single thing to say. My sister recognised him and turned back to say hello. She called to me, saying it's so and so, but I just stood where I was until they had exchanged pleasantries. I believe he also offered his condolences on the loss of my mother. It was about a year after she had died; he and my mother were genuinely fond of each other. What happened in the intervening years for Maestro is pure speculation, and it was not until the year 2007 that we formally met again.

Someone who I grew up with phoned me one day in 1998/99 and told me that Maestro was in the newspapers. Apparently he was under investigation by the police, I forget what particular crime he is said to have committed. I remember laughing and thinking that she had to be joking. Maestro was far too sensible and level headed to ever be involved in something sinister or criminal. He was from a well to do family who lived in the Caribbean; an intelligent man who had a lot going for him, including running his own business. What on earth could that be about? I decided that someone was having a joke at my expense. I remembered that Maestro liked to tell far-fetched stories, including jumping over several articulated lorries, and so decided this was probably one of those tales. To this day I do not know whether there was any truth or accuracy to the rumour.

In 2007 I attended the 100th birthday celebration of Rose Caines, a friend of my mother. We all call her Tanty, and she is a great-aunt, a godmother and grandmother to many in Leeds and Canada. She's a wise and loving old lady, and I am fond of her. It was a great family reunion as my siblings from Canada and family friends from abroad were all in attendance at this event. I enjoyed the day, but knew something was wrong, when my sisters began to avoid me. I was told a lot later that they were embarrassed and deeply hurt by some of the comments which had been put for me to repeat in my sleep. I was rejected by the family, and essentially shunned from the family group. One wonders how they knew what I said in my sleep, when I was totally ignorant of the fact that I was making inappropriate and disgusting remarks. Nevertheless that is what took place.

In the evening of the 100th birthday celebration the same person who had told me of Maestro's previous plight/brush with the law, told me that he was outside; and also warned me that he was married. I was totally stunned, I had not seen this man since approximately 1994, and here he was about to walk back into my life. Maestro walked through the door, the dance floor was empty and I stood in the middle of the floor, mouth agape as he walked directly towards me. The years had been kind and although he was overweight he looked handsome and brought back images of a dashing knight in shining armour. While in conversation Maestro asked me if I had married and I responded that I hadn't. I asked him if he had ever married and he said no. He asked me what I wanted to drink and then bought me an orange juice. Oh! I forgot to mention that he once again proposed marriage, I was too surprised to respond. Later that evening he dropped one of my sisters' and I back to another sisters' house, and then took me back to the place where I was staying.

He was a little distant, not quite as I had remembered, but I suppose the intervening years had caused him to be cautious. What I now suspect is that my sisters had asked him to deal with the situation. There was the general awareness that I needed to move from where I was living, and it's possible that he was the one who they had asked to be supportive in getting me out of the house. There were perhaps barriers of different kinds that needed to be dealt with, but my siblings could no longer ignore the fact that I was being abused and used inappropriately.

In the months that followed and the telephone conversations which we had, I fell madly in love with Maestro again. I knew I had to be careful, the warning echoed that he was married, yet we communicated and laughed and it was like old times again. Maestro has a very comfortable manner and can be very amusing. I enjoyed his company and his witty repartee. However after he spent Christmas of 2007 with me, everything went pear shaped. Mummy, as Maestro is also referred, became angry and his rage seemed to know no bounds. He started to be abusive, screaming and shouting profanity in the street at me, and saying the most vulgar and filthy things. Maestro essentially became Mr Abuse and not Mr Wonderful. It is my contention that because of his violent outbursts and behaviour that the inappropriate and vulgar remarks were repeated and perpetuated for far longer than they should have been.

Someone once claimed that he was trying to be supportive of me, but actually made things much worst, a comment which is a little patronising, but certainly true. Was this a man whom I had previously hurt getting his revenge, it seems to be the most likely explanation.

Revenge or the action or behaviour of repaying someone who you may believe has wronged you is not uncommon. In my experience, whilst the Holy Bible says do not repay evil for evil, but repay evil for good, man often acts to appease his ego. Revenge takes many forms. In saying this perhaps we can briefly consider 'Magazine'. The word Magazine has been bandied about for the last few years, and can be placed in this context.

What is Magazine, is it a pseudonym for someone or a nickname? Does it have other associative meanings, or is it applied in some other context? Magazine seems to connote dirtiness, and by a glance or other signification is passed on. The suggestion is that the person is a slut, either through a lack of cleanliness or hygiene. It may imply that their sexual practices are basically immoral and this is someone who should in no way be valued. The phrase was coined several years ago, and I believe arose from a situation between myself and a lodger I then had. Periodically, over the years I took in lodgers.

This particular lodger was a young man, nineteen years of age. He moved into my home because he was attending the local university. He often spent the week by me, and the weekends at his parents' home. We got on quite well together, and one day he confided that he was a homosexual. He hadn't told his parents, but felt the need to start sharing the information. Basically he was 'coming out' and was testing other people's reactions. I'm fairly broadminded, and reassured him that he had to be true to himself. I encouraged him to tell his parents, and at some point he probably did.

When he graduated from university and left my home, I became aware from his mail that he had been ordering a gay magazine. The magazine showed other gay men either naked or scantily dressed. I suppose it's the gay equivalent to Playboy. I wasn't pleased and forwarded it on to his parents' home address in Thornton Heath, which was the only forwarding address I had for him. I also cancelled the subscription when it became evident that he had no intention of stopping it from coming to my home. I would throw the offending magazines that arrived into the bin, and thought that was the end of the matter. This occurred around 1996, however despite that, to this day 'Magazine' is still used as a way to offend or disrespect me. It seems that a neighbour took offence when I asked him to stop using my drive as a thoroughfare, and to gain revenge ordered another subscription of the gay magazine. It arrived at my address for years and was promptly put in the bin, which is where it belongs.

Relationships are complex things, especially the one between a man and woman. I don't know if you have ever read the book 'Men are from Mars, Women Are from Venus', which gives a great deal of insight into the difficulties the sexes have in communicating effectively with each other. The book's central premise is that men were born on Mars and have a totally different language and ways of communicating to women who were born on Venus. The author argues that men are often more logical and analytical. They get their sense of self achievement from being task oriented and self-reliant. Women on the other hand are more intuitive and get a sense of self through relationships. Our connections are to other people, instead of priding ourselves on our self-reliance. For a woman asking for help and offering it is a compliment. This is a summarised version of the book, which looks in depth at communication between the sexes.[14]

The book further argues that men tend to be compartmentalised, like a chest of drawers; work and its concerns in one drawer, relationships in another drawer, sports in a third drawer, and so on. All of the various parts of a man's life being split off from each other. Women it is argued are far less compartmentalised and everything is connected to everything else. Most women can't get romantic when there's some unresolved anger or frustration with their partner. Men often don't see what the two things have to do with each other. My argument here is that when Maestro, spent the night flirting at a party with a friend of my sister he seemed unaware of the hurt and embarrassment that he was causing me. Thus his expectation that I would later be able to respond to his gestures of affection were not only an indication of his insensitivity to my feelings, but that he was missing communication cues.

'Men are from Mars, Women Are from Venus' further argues that when a man is under stress he generally distract himself, as a way of relaxing. This may involve heading for the football pitch or burying himself in television or in reading a newspaper. Most men are self-reliant and competitive, so to ask for help is a weakness. He will first want to solve the problem by himself, so he heads for his cave. A woman on the other hand will call her friends, sisters, confidantes to discuss the problem.

In a relationship between the sexes there are needs. A man's need is for respect, trust, acceptance, appreciation, admiration, approval and encouragement. Women also need the same thing, but in addition need to be cherished, that is to receive tender care, understanding, devotion, validation and reassurance. Just as a man needs to be needed, we as women need to be protected.

> "Husbands, love your wives, just as Christ also loved the church and gave Himself for her . . ."[15]

The analogy between Christ's love for the church, and a man's love for his wife demonstrates the way in which a man should care for his wife. Essentially Christ's love for the church was a sacrificial love, a tender love, and a love that is committed to acting in the church's best interest. God doesn't just want men to love their wives like they love sports, he wants a man to love his wife in a way that makes her feel cherished and very special, to love her and put her needs and desires above his own. The Holy Bible in 1 Peter 3:7 :

> "Husbands, likewise, dwell with them (wives) with understanding, giving honour to the wife, as to the weaker vessel . . . (since she is a woman). [16]

The analogy is to consider women as a china cup, fragile, delicate and far more valuable. We treat our china with tenderness and gentleness, because of its fragility and value. In reading the above two passages from the Bible, I wondered about fidelity and faithfulness in a committed relationship, such as in a marriage. My experience cannot be discussed in the context of a marriage, at least not a union which would be recognised by the church. However, I am aware of friends who have strayed outside of their marriages to conduct love affairs, and sometimes sexual liaisons with people other than their spouses.

I was recently made aware of a couple who I have known since I was a young woman who experienced a time in their marriage when one of the partners was unfaithful. They have been married for many years and their children are now grown up with a family of their own. The wife in this particular situation had everything she wanted. She had a beautiful home, a family, a great husband, but she felt she should be happier, something was missing. She decided it must be a lack of something in her career, so perhaps if she took an additional course, she would be able to develop her self-esteem, as well as make more of a financial contribution to the home. She persuaded her husband that she needed to go abroad to study for this course. It of course meant leaving her husband and children, but the sacrifice would be worthwhile in the fullness of time.

Whilst abroad, she realised her desires were being reawakened in this new environment. She was outside of the marital home, and exposed to contact with 'a new man'. She started an affair with him and felt alive once more. The justification for this affair, could have been her husband's past behaviour. Most husbands are unaware that their wives are having affairs. Their lack of suspicion is typically due to their wife's disinterest in sex, and in their belief that their wife is a 'good girl'. It is important to remember that a man would also trust his wife. I have no wish to either moralise or to pass judgement; my only comment is that the sexual liaison took place with her sister's partner.[17]

The couple in this particular instance chose to stay married. The affair was ended by the outrage of her sister, who made the sexual affair publicly known to all; her husband was forgiving and they worked to ensure their marriage survived. The reason that some women will give for having extra marital affairs is a search for self. Unfortunately not all marriages survive infidelity.

Interestingly enough a woman who has lost interest in sex with her husband, and who views sex as a job, not unlike washing the dishes, may ultimately stray.

Sex should be perceived as an expression of love between a man and his wife. In some circumstances If a wife feels violated when touched by their husband, they may also be fearful that their disinterest in sex will lead to a breakdown in the marriage. If they then experience re-awakened desires by an encounter outside of the marital relationship the women will give a lot of importance to these encounters. It may be a person in the work environment, or could be a friend or acquaintance of the husband.

The feeling of being 'alive' may be expressed, as some of these women have not felt any sexual desire for a long time. Many experience guilt and regret at the loss of the "good girl" status which is replaced by the status of being unfaithful and a "bad girl". [18]

I have never been married nor have I ever had a sexual relationship with two people at the same time. I have been in a situation where I was dating someone who was living with someone else and I therefore dated someone else as well, however I only have sex with one person at a time and often leave months or years, before another sexual encounter. I cannot speak for Maestro, I know when we were young people that he was unfaithful, nowadays I cannot speak about his fidelity.

CHAPTER FOUR

DYSFUNCTIONAL RELATIONSHIPS

Sunday 28ᵗʰ August 2011

St John's Methodist Church, USVI

I arrived late at church this morning, and it seems as if everything stopped when I arrived. The church is very lively with many musicians playing the saxophone, piano, drums, guitars and cymbals; making a joyous noise to the Lord. That's probably why I felt very conspicuous as I walked in aware that I was well over half an hour late and the actual sermon had begun. The service was inspiring and reminded me of my faith in Jesus Christ. I am a believer, a born again Christian. Two phrases which struck a note are that we are to be joyful in hope and patient in affliction.

Am I a lukewarm christian? Attending church when it serves my best interests? I hope not. I am not a regular church goer for a variety of reasons, but I do hold christian values and principles. My own views can be discussed from the perspective of an academic's interest in religion together with living, as far as possible a christian life with christian principles. One particular premise which I find interesting is Karl Marx which argues that 'religion is the opium of the masses'. Essentially, Marx is arguing that a prime purpose of religion is to domesticate the poor. Religion, he argues, is used to detract the proletariat from the economic realities of their lives. This is perhaps a little cynical, and perhaps not relevant in contemporary society.[19]

The dichotomy between religion and psychology is that one is the science of human behaviour, whilst the other is the moral and social mores by which a civilized society socializes and ensures conformity to its rules and regulations. Moreover, there are it is argued different types of religion, 'institutionalized religion and personal religion'. Institutionalized religion is said to be a religious group or organisation, whereas personal religions are those where an individual is practising an alternative religion. This may refer for instance to 'spiritualist' churches where some who attend are said to be psychics or mediums.[20] I have no wish to moralize or tell others how to live their lives; however I have come to learn through the reading of my bible and through bible studies that these practices were frowned upon. In *Leviticus (19:31)* we are told we should:

> "Give no regard to mediums and familiar spirits: do not seek after them to be defiled by them: I am the Lord your God."[21]

Prior to becoming a born again christian I was encouraged by someone who I grew up with to consult the tarot line, if I needed some insight into the future. I have come to recognise as a more mature christian that while it may seem to be a harmless endeavour similar to reading one's horoscope that we are warned against this practice in the Holy Bible. This particular person also advocates that she is a medium and able to communicate with the dead. As a previous friend I have warned her of the dangers involved in these things, they are not of God. *In 1 Corinthians 13:11* we learn that we are to act in a mature manner:

> "When I was a child, I spoke as a child; I understood as a child, I thought as a child, but when I became a (woman), I put away childish things." [22]

Other proponents have added their views to the discussion about man's need for religion in his life. Freud argues that religious beliefs are at best infantile and somewhat neurotic, whilst authoritarian religion is perceived as dysfunctional, its only purpose being to alienate man from himself. This criticism is perhaps a little harsh, and I have adopted a more balanced approach in my own life.

In most religions God is considered to be perfect, omnipotent and omnipresent and his wish is for us to be likewise perfect. The rationale is that if we too achieve perfection we may become one with God, not God. Our views of God are important as it may well embody our goals and it directs our social interaction. The traditional view taken from The Holy Bible, Genesis is that man was placed on earth to be God's ultimate creation.

This has been replaced over time to include those who see the universe as a more abstract representation of nature, in some instances even arguing that God can be perceived as an abstract representation of nature's force. This is aptly delineated in the poetry of Wordsworth and Blake. Wordsworth's poetry celebrates man and nature and indicates that 'the individual's soul is touched by Divinity putting aside the petty needs of ego and materialistic distractions.[23] On the other hand Blake's poems in the book *'Songs of Innocence and Experience Shewing the Two Contrary States of the Human Soul* indicates that human nature and society can be assessed through symbolic representations. For instance the tiger represents mature man whose soul may be corrupt and the lamb (which also conveys an imagery of Christ) as humble, gentle and as yet uncorrupted.[24] I reiterate I have very orthodox christian views, and whilst I delight in the beauty of nature, this is in my opinion the creation of our heavenly father.

As previously said there are several schools of thought regarding the psychology of religion. Another exponent is Allport who makes a distinction beween mature religion and immature religion. The argument is that mature religion is dynamic, open-minded and able to maintain links between inconsistencies. In contrast immature religion is self-serving and generally represents the negative stereotype that people have about religion.

Recently he changed the terminology to intrinsic and extrinsic religion. Overall he argues that some religious belief is important in our lives, and we may respond to it positively or negatively. The notion of a personal religion and being able to make conscious choices about our relationship with God is what he purports determines the type of christian we may become. It's interesting to note at this point that the *Holy bible; Matthew 5:48* tells us what our behaviour should be, that is to be Christ like, and to emulate Christ's behaviour.[25]

"Therefore you shall be perfect, just as your father in heaven is perfect."

Finally, I would like to briefly mention Fromm's analysis of religion. In his view human beings need a stable frame of reference or a foundation in which to discuss our existence about how the universe was formed. Essentially, he argues that we crave answers to questions about how we came into being that no other source of knowledge can answer. It is important however that a sense of free will be given in order for religion to appear healthy.[26]

It is in this context that I would like to explore my understanding of dysfunctional relationships. Given, that I have a sound foundation on which I base my religious views, that is the Holy Bible, and that these views have encouraged a healthy life style, that is abstinence from tobacco and alcohol; I would argue that I have a physically and emotionally healthy way of life.

My prayer life and social support network have encouraged a healthy and optimistic outlook on life, and my return to meditation also has physiological benefits. Having evaluated what I considered a balanced and healthy emotional life and the ability to sustain healthy relationships, I want to take this opportunity to explore dysfunctional relationships.

Dysfunctional relationships are said to be those which do not perform their appropriate function, that is, they do not emotionally, support participants, foster communication positive or otherwise between those in the relationship, or prepare those in the relationship for life in a larger world. Instead notions of jealousy and envy are perpetuated to justify certain types of controlling behaviour and at times stories are invented to ensure that others outside of the relationship think badly of the other. This might take the form of being sexually inappropriate or other myths.

Within dysfunctional relationships, and I would argue that the relationship between Lamp-post and myself comes within this category; there is a lack of empathy and understanding. She seems unaware of the boundaries and in addition deliberately misinforms, and is abusive towards me. For instance, she shouts and screams and at times makes filthy comments, she certainly feels the need to control my behaviour by shouting 'apologise'. It may be that she is displeased by something I am doing, and therefore screams that I need to apologise to her. Her ego is such that she seems to constantly need to prove that she is the one in control.[27]

Recently I learned that Lamp post and I had shared a sexual partner, I was told by a previous friend. Apparently it's common knowledge, I refer specifically to a reference that was made at a family celebration. The comment was 'bump the pussy'. This rather crude description is, it would seem how a particular family member perceived of and described the occurrence. Someone else once said that 'she is a back stabber', I only now realise why the comment was made.

My understanding of the situation is as follows. It seems that years ago she and George had a flirtation. He had just moved into the area and by all accounts she managed to fit him in or have sex with him as well as her current lover. I was introduced to him by her and I said that I quite liked him. At that point she never indicated that she wanted to have a relationship with him or even just have him as a lover. There was no indication from her that this man was a' no go area'; which of course he was. We both visited him at his own invitation one christmas and he was perfectly civil to both of us. I did not receive one single clue that they had previously been lovers. As neighbours he even came across the road one day and left a christmas card for both of us. Over the years because he was friendly I became friends with this man and would pop in occasionally for a cup of tea, just as friends. He visited me on a few occasions once for dinner. We started and maintained a friendship for several years.

When years later he made an approach towards me indicating that he wanted more than friendship; we did not sleep together immediately, and my sister was my closest friend at the time. I told her, what was happening; that George seemed interested in having a relationship with me so she knew it would mean that we would eventually become lovers. I cannot believe that she did not say then or previously that she and this man had been lovers. After we had sex, he tried to tell me, but it came out wrong and I did not react too well to what he was saying. My interpretation was that he fancied her, not that he had actually had sex with her.

Given the way he behaved when he came to a concert all those years ago I now understand other people's reactions. He accepted an invitation which I had extended to him knowing full well that he could not in the circumstances continue the relationship. I am now fully aware that I have walked around England in total ignorance for years not fully understanding some of the snide remarks or references which were made with regards to George. One particular snub was the inference that I should be wearing either cheap or second hand clothing. I now totally understand the rude and inappropriate comments; previously I was too stupid to understand.

Lamp post and George are equally to blame, he knew and should have said something prior to having sex with me, and she knew and should have also have said before the event. I remember him making comments like he didn't get enough sex; which is a totally unsuitable remark. He should never have had the opportunity of having sex with me, and I feel totally defiled when I realise how vulnerable and exposed I was left by Lamp post.

There was a good friend of mine named Steve who I use to play squash with, who she apparently fancied. She asked me if I was interested in him, and I said not in that way. He was a good friend, and I had no wish to change the relationship. They had a brief fling which I believe ended badly, however she was given the information she needed so she could make an informed choice. My argument is that I was denied the opportunity of making an informed choice.

When I ask myself how could this have happened, how could I not have known that Lamp post and George had been lovers? It is I believe one of those well kept secrets that everyone knows. She told other people not to tell me: I don't want her to know is what she would say. "sshh!"

> "Do not correct a scoffer, lest he hate you. Rebuke a wise man, and he will love you. Give instruction to a wise man and he will be still wiser." [28]

Just as my relationship with Lamp post is dysfunctional and we no longer speak to each other, I am aware of two other sisters who have been lovers with the same man. S and

J are sisters and good friends; however J thought she should have any man that she wanted. She was in a position where she had a choice as she knew her sister was with this man. This man however, looked good to her, and although he was with her sister, and they were practically living together, that did not make a difference. S became pregnant for her man, but he eventually leaves her for her sister. After a time the man shares the sisters who squabble and cuss each other, and basically stab each other in the back.

My contention is that my choice was taken away. If two women equally like a man, and one has already made a claim on that man, then the other should back off. Many men will play with both women if they are given the opportunity. Thus it is important to have integrity and ensure that you have all the facts at your disposal and share the facts if necessary.

It is easy to blame others for what I perceive as my misfortunes. However, it would not do much good to adhere to the 'blame culture'. My siblings did this and my siblings said that. Pity me, poor me, how could you do that to me. That is certainly one perspective or stance, but my own particular attitude is that it's good to take responsibility for one's own actions and not merely say it wasn't me or it wasn't my fault. We are all accountable for our actions and interactions. I am accountable for repeating and discussing some comments which are unkind and have hurt other people's feelings. For this I apologize as I have no wish to repeat what I may have said to cause the hurt. I have to ultimately take responsibility for being lovers with George. I believe however as previously said that I was denied the opportunity of making an informed choice.

Recently I watched a television programme called Dr Phil where the host of the programme counsels people who are in dysfunctional relationships. There was a family on the programme who were experiencing difficulty because the man had sex with his wife's sister. It was a relationship which involved him telling his sister-in-law that he loved her, and perhaps there had initially been plans to end the marriage. The pain and hurt caused in situations such as this knows no bounds, as this man thought he could have his cake and eat it. The reality is that he has destroyed any previous trust which existed between himself and his wife. In addition two sisters are no longer able to be supportive or communicate positively with each other.

The marriage is not at an end; however the wife nags and checks on him constantly because she is no longer able to believe in his fidelity.

CHAPTER FIVE

MY SIBLINGS

Tuesday 6th September 2011

Villa, St John, USVI

I moved from the apartment into a Villa today. It's very beautiful, tranquil and expansive. It has two bedrooms, but I'm just paying for the use of one. It's peaceful and like living in paradise. Its cooler this evening than yesterday but I missed this evening's sunset. Yesterday's was absolutely beautiful the colours which spread over the sea were different shades of reds interspersed with billowy clouds. It was picture perfect; it's the sort of scene that you see on a postcard. Tonight I can hear the crickets in the background and am told there is a strong scent of jasmine, my sense of smell is marred by my allergies. There are lights on in a few houses and just outside a few boats are docked in the marina. The setting is perfect to continue writing my memoirs.

As a teacher of english literature I often analyse the different characters in a novel in terms of their attitude and various preoccupations. To some extent this is applied in my assessment of human beings whom I come into contact with on a daily basis. We all use our own judgement and intuition to understand people in our immediate social worlds. In the play The Wild Duck by Ibsen, the wild duck is presented as a symbol. It is a symbol which gives a reader some insight into the various characters in the play and also some understanding of their differing preoccupations.

Essentially the Wild Duck symbolises dysfunction. The bird itself has a damaged wing and is a little lame in one foot. The wild duck lives in the attic where it can retreat from the reality of the everyday harshness of the real world into its own imagined idealised place. As the play unfolds we learn that the family Ekdal's have many secrets, and the happy home which is initially presented is not the reality of their lives. There is deceit, pretence, hypocrisy, avoidance, and a distinct lack of the truth in their relationships with each other.[29]

I am painfully aware that my siblings and I are imperfect; moreover I recognise that in writing and having this book published that I am exposing myself and other members of the family to criticism. Some justification of this is that over the years my siblings have been discussed, by others, in a less than favourable manner. Additionally, I genuinely believe that if the rift is to be healed, that it is necessary for me to make my views known. Forgiveness necessitates sharing and understanding of what has taken place. Essentially I am arguing that we all need to acknowledge and understand the hurts, slights and inappropriate remarks which have been made and repeated throughout the years. Also In writing this chapter, I felt the need to highlight that our parents, especially my father encouraged us to love and be supportive of each other. I refer to both my actual father as well as our heavenly father. Ours was a family which was well respected in the Leeds community in Yorkshire and I grew up in a supportive loving family environment. As with all siblings, especially as we grew older there were differences and arguments. I distinctly recall my parents distress if as sisters we were less than kind to each other. Such as one of my sisters' telling me she needed to pour bleach over me, as it was quote 'said to kill all known germs'.

Or another sisters' act of kindness when I had a bad cold, in rubbing me all over with fiery jack; my skin was inflamed for days. The joy of having older sisters knows no bounds. On a more serious note I was protected and cared for by having older sisters; and this pattern of looking after each other, and caring for one another was passed on by me to my younger siblings. I suppose my role in the family as the fourth child or a middle child is somewhat tenuous, it is certainly fraught with difficulties.

A common idea that my two younger siblings use to share was that despite my mother's view that there were three big ones and three little ones; I had aspirations to be one of the big ones. As such there were four big ones and two little ones. A view which they perpetuated for years. As a middle child I was fortunate in learning how to care for those younger than myself, and ensuring they took their responsibility for sharing in tidying up in the home. This in itself caused arguments; and I remember years later they both ganged up on me, and said I use to force them to do the housework and simply sit back and supervise them. This is not true, but it's interesting to note how people remember things differently. Perhaps in getting their revenge for any imagined slights they sought to supervise and dominate me in later life. This is known as the Edna syndrome.

Once I use to receive a great deal of positive attention as a family member. I was often actively involved in supporting others whether it was in an emotional or financial capacity. Over the years however, after the death of my mother things changed, and I began to receive a lot of negative attention from some of my siblings. There was no longer any sensitivity to my feelings and views and some of the comments made were unsuitable, inappropriate, too familiar and unchristian. My siblings became abusive and failed to realise that some of the boundaries in regards to discussing my life were missing. I would further argue that when they recognised there were boundaries they were disregarded, and that they failed to communicate at an early stage that I was repeating inappropriate remarks in my sleep. I know I've been speaking by the quality of sleep which I've had but don't often remember what I've repeated. I also believe that someone should have approached me directly and told me that I had shared a sexual partner with Lamp post. Some of the information to which I was denied access is absolutely vital, and some of it relates to basic health and safety.

When writing in hindsight with more information it is easy to say I should have done this or I should have done that, or they should have behaved in certain ways. Today, as I sit down and analyse my life I want to make it clear that I do not blame anyone for the problems or difficulties I have encountered in life. These misfortunes are to an extent part of life and should be viewed as such, but I have to make it clear that I am very angry that information I should have been made aware of was withheld from me for years. There cannot be any justification other than shame and embarrassment for discouraging others from letting me know what had taken place or was taking place.

I learned a few years ago that people, I don't know who they are, had a key to my backdoor. I have repeated this information throughout the book because to me it is inconceivable that anyone's privacy could be invaded in this way, and over such a long period of time. I was then made aware that someone had spoken to my sister about this some time ago. One of her friends had told her I needed to be warned that people were coming into my property through the back door. Unfortunately this information was never communicated. I couldn't hear anything and didn't suspect that this was happening.

I strongly believe that I needed to be warned a long time ago that my home was accessible, it's in no way a laughing matter. The information was finally made available through a work colleague a few years later, and they are the ones who encouraged me to change all the locks. A situation like this is very dangerous, and irrespective of what your feelings are for your sibling you should ensure that she is aware that a key has allegedly been found and that the neighbours/strangers are entering your home. Instead of warning me this sibling used the information about people accessing my property to imply that I was a slut; which is not the case. She would come into my home and say something like 'nasty her up'; and then proceed to wipe her dirty feet all over my carpet. I can give no explanation or justification for her behaviour.

On one occasion although I had locked the bedroom door in the morning I found the lock had been broken, which meant that someone had been in the property, and had actually been in my bedroom. I cannot tell you how frightened I was when I realised how vulnerable I had been during the night. I can only think that I had been asked where I kept the spare key for the bedroom and answered in my sleep. I do not believe I sleep walk, and instead think that the key was used. Or a more obvious alternative is that the lock was broken in order to gain access.

"Love you back" which implies that you only have to tell her you love her and she will open the backdoor is a misnomer, and it also does not refer to any part of my anatomy. It's also interesting to note that whosoever had access to the house, when they realised they were locked out, stole my keys and cut another one. It seems someone needed to have access to me by any means necessary. A friend once tried to wise me up on this, but it is only over the years that I have realised the point she was making.

Illegal entry to my property and the constant reporting and monitoring of me still causes me concern. I am not a criminal and am not involved in any anti-social or political factions which would make me an enemy of the state, yet as I move from place to place the same people follow me and ensure that my reputation is damaged. It is almost as if in injuring my character, whosoever has issues or a need to misuse me in some way maintains some control in my life. Another piece of information which I believe is vital, and if shared earlier would certainly have encouraged me to find somewhere else to live is that I was trained to repeat information in my sleep. Over the years many availed themselves of my services to disrespect whosoever they had issues with and to misuse me to the extent that I would repeat anything even if it were about my own self. I refer only to speaking at this point as I have no knowledge of any other abuse whilst asleep in my home.

I was often interviewed by the neighbours and it seems outsiders about my personal, emotional and financial affairs. I reiterate I was also trained to repeat, sometimes the most disgusting comments including swear words in my sleep. This I would argue is part of the psychological phenomenon previously alluded to. Not only was I encouraged to repeat other people's comments, so that they could tell other people exactly what they thought of them, they then ensured that Bev was blamed. I was often placed in the embarrassing situation of listening to the comments of others who were discussing what had taken place while I was asleep the previous night. At times I objected, but for the most part I listened to what was taking place as it was the only way that I would know what had happened. Perhaps that was perceived as permission to continue, or that I was in some way complicit in what was taking place. This is not the case, I did not consciously ever give consent to my personal affairs being publicly discussed. On the occasions when I tried to silence the perpetrator, they would ensure they continued the discussion, but that I could no longer hear what they were saying. Travelling to work and listening to the information being made available, either through someone's mobile phone, a neighbour or associate following me, or some other means of communication was to put it mildly humiliating. I am not sure what the law says in this regard, but it seems to contravene the Human Rights Act 1998, a person's right to privacy.

Whilst working at the University during 2006 to 2008, I was made aware that I fell asleep, both at work and also in the streets. When this happened it seemed that people would deliberately interfere with my clothes and touch me inappropriately. Rape and sexual abuse were imminent, and to ensure it could not either happen again or happen for the first time, I needed to be told/made aware that I fell asleep. I don't know how long this situation has gone on for, but am aware that I needed to be told directly that this is what was happening, i.e. you are falling asleep or dozing off for a few minutes at a time.

There are a number of factors why I fall asleep, one is that I have an under active thyroid, for which I take medication, and the correct dosage needs to be taken. Secondly, the blood pressure tablets which I also take were counteracting the effects of my thyroid medication. Thus I needed to change the blood pressure medication to ensure that it enabled good functioning, i.e. not falling asleep. If I were aware that I fell asleep, I would not 'wander off' to lonely roads/places and would ensure my visibility. I believe a family member was made aware that the medication I was taking might be unsuitable and could be causing me to under function. I have now been made aware of this, and will ensure that the correct medication is taken, thus falling asleep is not now as likely.

A few of my colleagues also made me aware that I really couldn't hear properly and was missing background and other sounds. My family must have realised this for years. I would just mention that some took this opportunity to speak for me. I have no wish for you to speak for me; I am articulate and able to communicate on my own behalf. I have no wish to be patronised and would encourage my siblings to communicate with me directly, ensuring I can hear them. This comment relates to all, not just my siblings. I am listening and am more likely to hear you as I am awake, and the medication taken for my blood pressure and under-active thyroid are correct.

I would also hear you more clearly if pulverising did not take place. Pulverising is the process of making the loudest possible sounds, including the slamming of doors, banging of windows, banging on the walls, stamping of feet and may also include screaming and shouting at the top of your voice. The purpose of this is to intimidate me so that I do not hear as accurately as I should. I believe it's a technique used with prisoners of war to ensure their compliance and obedience.

In some instances I was deliberately kept awake or woken from a deep sleep by someone making loud noises and hitting the wall, ceiling, banging bins, etc. The purpose it is claimed was to ensure that I did not repeat inappropriate remarks. I suspect the converse is true, and someone needed me to be half awake so that I could be misused. I say this in the knowledge that all that happened when I was constantly woken throughout the night was that I was more tired and more susceptible to abuse, as I would inevitably fall asleep in the day, and dribble. At this point I would ask that you stop waking me up. I do not require an alarm clock and I have no wish to be awoken. I would also appreciate it if you would stop monitoring and discussing what I say whilst asleep.

Finally, Maestro drew to my attention the fact that I actually speak out loud without realising it. He calls it 'dribbling', meaning that I am speaking my thoughts out loud. (It means I am asleep). I cannot hear myself when I do this, and appreciate that he has ensured that' babbly' is aware of it. I hope this happens more infrequently than it did, however, if I am speaking out loud please feel free to point it out to me in a tactful manner.

I would like to reiterate that I was expelled from the family group in 2007 because of the disgusting remarks, which had been 'put'. That is people started to come along and would ask a neighbour to repeat the comments to me when I was asleep. The rationale presumably is that I could then repeat it and be blamed for the comments. The comments were about my own mother; apparently previously I had been encouraged to admit untruths about my father.

To ensure the accuracy of the information, I have begun taping myself in my sleep. I have no evidence to date that I have repeated offensive remarks, but I have only recently begun to check. I do not disbelieve that I have repeated inappropriate remarks whilst sleeping, but would point out that there are many occasions when the comments are actually other people's who then blame me for the comments or previously recorded comments are being replayed.

Prior to being thrown out of the family, I would argue that I had been marginalised for years. One particular relative has been very disrespectful for a long time, and has used offensive and abusive language to me, including wishing me dead; presumably I had offended him in some way. There was also a perception of me was as something of an 'oddball, someone who doesn't quite fit in with the rest of the group. I was no longer involved or rather should say was deliberately excluded from my sibling affairs, gossip and so forth. I was no longer in the know, and not encouraged to participate in 'family' life.

However in 2009 when I was living in Wellingborough I was visited by one of my siblings. Two of my siblings have been less than kind and we have not spoken to each other since 2008. In my opinion they have both behaved abysmally for the short time I was living in Leeds, including shouting and screaming and encouraging people to physically abuse me; I believe the expression used is 'clat (hit) her'. In addition some of the most offensive remarks about my private parts were made, including a public discussion of the men I am supposed to have previously had sex with. I was also accused of stealing all of the money from the bank account in St Kitts.

Actually it was initially my account but I was encouraged to add one of my sisters' name in the event that something happened to me. I think the name 'stupidee 'is quite fitting in this instance. This information should be transposed to one of my sister's emptying the bank account in St Kitts, leaving something like ten dollars in the account. Fortunately a friend living on the island was able to assist with accommodation, so at least I had somewhere to stay. Many of the comments made by my siblings and repeated over time have caused me immense difficulty, and to say that some of the comments are unsuitable and even dangerous is to under estimate the impact that they have had in my life. I dare not refer to the remarks which were repeatedly made about my personal hygiene.

As I was saying one of my relatives showed up outside of the apartment in Wellingborough and instructed me to re-join the family. I believe her actual words were 'It's time to re-join the family.' I do not feel able to accept this invitation, and believe it's in everyone's best interest if I stayed outside of the sibling relationship. Perhaps it's my sensitive nature, but being sworn at and screamed at by several siblings has discouraged re-entry. Many of the comments I have made are common knowledge and can easily be verified if the need arose. It may seem fanciful or rather imaginative, but as they say truth is stranger than fiction. I have neither created nor embellished the incidents described.

Although I have lived on my own for the most part, my neighbours were encouraged to supervise, discipline or even fine me as the need arose. Fining took many forms but in essence the idea is to penalise me in some way if I do not fit in with their criteria. Falling asleep in the street gave others an opportunity to physically abuse me. I was given a routine by the neighbours which included waking me up, telling me to get a shower, to turn off the shower water and whether it was best to use the toilet before or after having a shower. Every aspect of my life was discussed and monitored this included what food to eat and what to buy at the supermarket, which is very offensive and incredibly disrespectful. In addition I became a business venture to some of my friends a means of making a profit. I suspect this is unlawful, but can only address it with full knowledge of how this operated, and exactly who was involved.

If my siblings intentions had been to be supportive in reality it became very invasive, intrusive and abusive. In addition workmen who were working on nearby houses were often encouraged to disrespect my private parts as I showered; my siblings are not responsible for this. I believe the original comments relate to 'masturbation' or its more crude form 'shagging' yourself in the shower. This I believe stems from a builder/carpenter whose behaviour, attitude and disgusting remarks live on to this day. I would like to take this opportunity of reassuring all that I do not need to be supervised, or have a routine established. Neither am I a threat to myself or anyone else. Overall I would argue that it is disrespectful and in no way amusing to treat or subjugate another human being in this manner.

The transatlantic slave trade came to an end well over 150 years ago and I should be grateful if you would note the following:

I DO NOT REQUIRE A BOSS OR MANAGER
I DO NOT REQUIRE A TRAINER
I DO NOT REQUIRE A CARER
I DO NOT REQUIRE AN ADVOCATE
I DO NOT REQUIRE A SUPERVISOR
I MAY REQUIRE A GOOD, HONEST CHRISTIAN HUSBAND

The 'Edna syndrome' doesn't work. It does not enable and encourage me to achieve my best. I do not want to be controlled as if I were child. I am not disabled and would hear clearly when taking the correct medication to control my blood pressure; and if inordinately loud noises were not made simply because I was in the vicinity. If encouraged my hearing, especially of background sounds would improve. It cannot possibly be in anyone's interest to deliberately tamper with my ability to hear most sounds to at least ninety percent audibility. Furthermore I would point out that I am not retarded, an idiot or a simpleton, nor do I have problems. These are myths which have been suggested to justify the behaviour of others. I am admittedly however, 'stupidee' and at times' fufu'.

I am a forgiving person and cannot see any reason to hold a grudge. I am fortunate in that I have been able to retire early and travel to North America and the Caribbean. I have a few writing projects in mind, and this together with some voluntary part-time teaching will keep me occupied and out of trouble. I am a committed christian, and hope to become more involved in a church which suits me and I suit them. This together with my interest in learning spanish and re-starting piano lessons will keep me busy for some time to come, God willing. In The Bible, James 4:13-15 we are taught to entrust all things to God, and trust in his judgement and not our own.

> "Come now, you who say, today or tomorrow we will go to such and such a city, spend a year there, buy and sell, and make a profit.' Whereas you do not know what will happen tomorrow. For what is your life? It is even a

vapour that appears for a little time and then vanishes away. Instead you ought to say 'If the Lord wills, we shall live and do this or that". [31]

In concluding this chapter I took many things into consideration. The premise of the book of celebrating motherhood was a major aspect, as I find myself in a situation where a wonderful mother's memory is still being disrespected. This is something which affects all family members, and it cannot be resolved by blaming each other, or passing it on to so and so, or by saying make it for Bev. I would gladly accept the comments, however, that does not satisfy some who wish to perpetuate the cycle of abuse. We need to work in harmony to resolve this situation and thereafter can continue on our separate paths.

How do we ensure that our parents memory survive in a constructive, respectful and positive manner? I have no wish for the public discussions which often take place and which include the most disgusting swear words to in any way make reference to either my mother or father. So in what ways do we ensure that the rift which exists between us does not perpetuate the disrespecting of our parents? What legal measures if any do we need to put in place so that I am no longer at risk of saying disgusting things to disrespect their memory? We need to think of the future generations to come. I have no children, but know my memory will live on. I would like to be remembered positively and not as the sibling who said disgusting things about her mother.

One of my siblings once said you cannot resolve conflict without discussion, it's important to communicate. Taking that on board, I would like to communicate that the family member who is still making the comments needs to stop, acknowledge the remarks and stop making them. I will take legal action to ensure that it is finally stopped for good. In addition I am now much wiser and aware of the inherent dangers and interference by others, and will take precautionary measures where I can to ensure my safety. I would just say I wish this had happened much earlier, but as they say better late than never. Incidentally, whilst outlining some of my concerns I would just mention that it has come to my attention that people often say 'make it for me', so that they can then discuss their own affairs on the pretext of being supportive of me. Once they have taken whatever the particular topic is and implicated me in whatever their particular issue is they then 'wipe their mouth' as if it has nothing to do with them. I would ask that you do not do this; I have no wish for you to act on my behalf or put disgusting responses for me to repeat in my sleep. Please do not interfere with me or discuss my affairs in any way.

In conclusion I would just mention that I have no wish to be followed all over the place, and will let you know where I am, please stop chasing me all over the world, please let me go. I would also point out that pulverising needs to stop, whosoever thinks they should be a 'hit man' should first attend the local police station. I really believe most of my grey cells have been knocked out, there are very few left, and I do need some in place so that I can perform certain basic tasks.

CHAPTER SIX

UP TO DATE 2009-2011

Friday 9th September 2011

Villa, St John, USVI

In attending in-service courses for teachers you are taught how to make your teaching effective and how to ensure that the students understand the lesson. Teachers are taught to tell and write the aims and objectives of a lesson on an OHP/chalkboard; this is what we are learning today, you would then teach what you said the lesson was about and at the end of the lesson evaluate that what you said you were going to teach is what you taught. Essentially you say what you are going to teach, teach it and then check that you've taught it. I've tried to fit that aim into writing this book. I am not teaching but sharing my experiences and hope that I have expressed what I wanted to say (stated my aims and objectives) taught it (clearly outlined my views) and finally checked that what I was telling you has been taught.

This is in no way meant to be patronising and I hope it is received in the spirit in which it is meant, as simply a tool which I am using to write and ensure understanding for all. In fact I have often argued that learning is a two way process and at times I have learned valuable lessons from my students. An example of this is when I was teaching a group of students the poem, *Half Past Two* as part of their GCSE course. It seems that some of the students, in an attempt to 'wise' me up, repeated the external comments which were simultaneously being made. The comments which were later repeated related to a fight I had, or really I should say when I was beaten up in the street, and ended up spending a few hours in jail.

I was on my way to a meeting at the college, when the people in the car in front of me started making the most offensive remarks and driving incredibly slowly. I honked my horn, but this served only to aggravate them, and the offensive remarks became worst. Finally the driver stopped dead in front of me, and came out of the car, swearing and cursing me. I got out and argued back, whereupon his wife jumped out of the passenger side of the car and proceeded to curse and spit on me. I responded, arguing back but not spitting, and was forcibly pushed in the bushes by both of them and kicked and hit. The police were called, but my inability to hear properly encouraged them to believe that I had struck first. One police officer encouraged me to let the matter go, but I needed to make the point. I had been attacked, and beaten up, which was evident from the scratches on my face, and if the only way that the perpetrators were going to go to jail is if I also went, then so be it. What lesson did I learn?

Primarily that I should have driven around them and avoided the conflict, that however, is in hindsight.

The poem *Half Past Two* by U A Fanthorpe, discusses doing something wrong. It is taken from a child's perspective, but I believe subtly makes the point that we are sinners and far from perfect.

"Once I did something wrong, I forget what it was . . ."[32]

What the child did wrong is something small and relatively insignificant. I would argue that in hitting back, this is similar to the minor crime committed by the child. We both did something wrong which was relatively insignificant. In my own particular situation what 'I did wrong' was to defend myself by hitting back, and I would argue that the punishment outweighs the crime. The child was left and actually forgotten because of a very small misdemeanour, and in addition made to feel extremely penalised because of the act. In applying this poem to my particular situation it might be argued that in hitting back I left myself open to police abuse, I was certainly left in a jail cell for far longer than required.

In addition the driving offence which I later acquired, offered those who had a wish to criminalise and control me, a greater opportunity to make demands on my life. In suggesting this the argument is if it can be proved that I am a criminal, then there will be a greater need for active police intervention. I would argue that this is what took place; I believe that a certain police officer was opportunistic and used my brief brushes with the law to advance his own career. This particular point of view has been suggested by many over the years, primarily by those who are watchdogs of the police; and as I delineate what took place, perhaps you can make your own judgement as to the motivation and intent of this particular police officer.

It was drawn to my attention that a particular police officer seemed overly interested in my affairs, to the extent that he began to discuss me in far too familiar a manner. Some may perceive of this as an attempt to capitalize on a situation which might promote his career. I did not at any stage ask nor did I give my permission for this particular officer to participate as actively as he did in my life. He apparently came to my place of work and told my colleagues that I was going to be arrested for an offence. This is untrue and it has never taken place however it served to alter other professionals' attitude and view of my character. I am not sure what his intentions were in doing this, but it served to ruin my credibility and reputation in the workplace. It seems he also has a tendency to warn fellow police officers that they should be aware that I am in the area, as I said the most disgusting things and could be aggressive. The implication was that I was a dangerous criminal, and should be actively monitored and my behaviour reported to the police on a regular basis. I am loathed to imply that racism might be at the heart of the interference which I have experienced at the hands of this police officer.

Not surprisingly other police officers have adopted a similar attitude, and responded to me in a disrespectful manner.

I was also discussed by this particular police officer as a slut, and he seemed to take great delight in discussing my private parts. I am aware that some police officers inferred from this that I was a prostitute. I would argue that a discussion of my anatomy is outside the boundaries of doing your job and should not take place. In addition coming into wherever I might be living in order to interview me whilst I am asleep is unlawful and should never again take place. I am fully aware that this particular police officer encouraged a landlord to let him have access to me so that he could say the most disgusting things to me, and ensure that I repeated the comments. This is unlawful entry and I believe is not regular police procedure.

After a time this particular police officer, began to follow me around the place and as I moved from town to town he would visit and discredit me in front of the general public and warn other police officers to be wary and ensure they took control of the situation. Similarly when I went abroad to visit an aunt and to live temporarily in St Vincent & the Grenadines the police were made aware of certain events which had previously occurred in my life. I would just state that the previous events were for the most part lies or referred to someone else, however, my inability to hear everything often ensured that I was implicated in something which had nothing to do with me.

I am referring specifically to an accusation which was made against me, which has never been substantiated and for which there are no foundations or proof. Allegedly I was supposed to have committed fraud or said to be involved in money laundering. This accusation was made and repeated whilst I was living in St Vincent and the Grenadines between September 2010 to May 2011. I would simply like to say that I have never committed fraud, I have never forged anything and I have never laundered money. I am not sure how this rumour was started, but rest assured it is untrue. I have neither tried to avoid or evade paying taxes. The only thing I needed to do was to file a tax return for the property which was recently sold. In the light of this I do hope that all accusations and innuendoes of wrongdoing are totally stopped.

I sometimes wonder if in making these accusations if revenge is a possible motivation? Is it that someone was trying to ensure that life abroad was made more difficult than it should be? I have certainly explored these possibilities, and often ask myself who would try to implicate me in such a thing and why? Whosoever is responsible has kept a relatively low profile, and I am thankful that they have failed in their endeavour.

Once I was made aware that someone had accused me of stealing my mother's pension. The comment is not true. I certainly use to collect it on her behalf, and if memory serves am the only one of the 'three' left in England who was willingly to do so. It's important for me that these things are made very clear as it is my reputation which is being brought into disrepute. My name and reputation are essentially the only thing which I have and it is that which is being disrespected.

"What's in a name-that which we call by any other name would smell as sweet"[33]

My name, both my surname and first name indicate something about me, it might be my identity, my personality or the name itself might have other associative meanings. My name is the way in which I am perceived by others and tells of my family history and origins. When you take my name and besmirch it you are doing damage not only to my character but also maligning my reputation. Essentially in ascribing negative connotations to my name you are damaging the essence of who I am. This is also the case when you make associations between my name and something which is essentially perceived as undesirable. I would like to take this opportunity of asking whosoever is involved in this to stop making such negative comments.

The bad name which I acquired while living for just a few months in Leeds ensured that I was glad to leave; and in February of 2009 I moved to Wellingborough a small town in Northamptonshire. January of the same year saw the inauguration of President Obama, the first black President of America. This was a proud moment in world history, and it encouraged a certain optimism for all our futures. It could, I believed, only be a matter of time before I got a job and was able to continue paying off the few debts which I still had. I was also in love, but that was another story.

I was pretty fortunate and found a really nice flat within a few days and moved in. The landlord seemed quite accommodating and when introduced to the other occupants of the building they all seemed fairly pleasant. It was mentioned that one of the occupants had close associations with the police, a relative of some sort, and as far as I was concerned this simply meant that the apartment building would be even safer.

The apartment building in Wellingborough was three storeys high, and the two single girls living on the ground floor were young but initially seemed friendly. There was a middle aged couple on the first floor who had a few grandchildren. I lived on the same floor as them on the opposite side of the building. The second floor was empty when I first moved in, but was rented for a short period of time after I had lived there for a few months.

The town itself was relatively small with only one high street and a small shopping mall. There were green fields surrounding the whole town and it was evident that it was a farming community. The population was diverse with a small African Caribbean community, a few Asians and the remaining population English. The previous mayor of the town was of African Caribbean descent and was a popular and respectable figure around the town.

I quickly got into a routine and found my way around the small town. However, it soon became apparent that I was not going to get on with the people in the apartment building as they were gossiping and discussing my affairs. I challenged them about it, only for an off duty police officer (someone's step-mom) to be called to have a quiet word with me in an unofficial manner. I persevered, it might be best to ignore them and get on with the task of job hunting. At first it seemed as if I might find work easily, but as time went on, although I was getting interviews, I was not getting the job. Apparently someone was making verbal references in addition to the usual standard written references. The verbal references implied that I was not a suitable person for the job. As the months went by the funds I had were dwindling and it was becoming increasingly difficult to pay my debts.

Something would have to be done, and it seemed like the best time to sell my house. I was out of work and not eligible for income support because of the large equity in the property. There was nothing else left to do but to put the house on the market. My property had been leased for a year, and there were about four months left before they would have to leave. I spoke to the tenants and told them of my intention to sell the property. I then contacted an estate agent and the house was placed on the market. Little did I know that hell was about to descend into my life. The estate agents obtained a buyer for the property quite quickly, and they indicated that they had no objection to waiting until the tenants moved.

Everything was going to plan, but my own lease on the flat had expired and the landlord seemed quite keen almost in a hurry for me to move. I was encouraged to leave the flat in Wellingborough when the lease expired in September 2009. I had not had particularly good experiences whilst living there, and I suppose my main achievement had been to successfully pass a word-processing course. I stayed for about seven months in total, but as the house was being sold it seemed sensible to return to London, so I could oversee the sale of my property. In the interim, what I did not know is that my mail was being intercepted, while I was living in Wellingborough, and that my mortgage lender wished to discuss new arrangements with regards to paying off the debt. Unfortunately I did not receive the necessary communications from them.

I moved back to Harrow in Middlesex, and experienced the worst physical abuse I have ever known. I was exposed to something which made me very ill, and I was unable to get out of bed for two days. In addition the police spent a lot of time outside of the address. Finally, I received a letter sent to the house, indicating that I would have to go to court, my lenders had placed an order to repossess the property as the full mortgage payments were not being made; and I had failed to make a reasonable proposal in order to settle the debt. I don't know why but I wasn't unduly worried, I had lived in the property for fifteen years, and over that time I had established a good relationship with my mortgage lender. In addition I was selling the property and the full debt would be realised in a few months. I suppose that's why the judge decided to give me some time, and delayed the possession order.

It is however, when the possession order was acquired that I also seem to gain a higher and more visible police presence. I am somewhat at a loss to know the reason for this. I asked the court staff for copies of the paperwork which had been sent to Wellingborough, and it is then, and only then that I realised that someone had been deliberately stealing my mail.

With this new information to hand it seemed like the end of the matter, as I was no longer ignorant to the fact that my lenders wanted either to make arrangements for the full monthly amount of the mortgage be paid or to pay off the whole debt by selling my house. The end seemed to be in sight and I believed it would only be a matter of time until the tenants moved out of the house. Unfortunately this was not the case as the tenants had their own agenda and refused to move, hell had descended into my life. I had to go through the whole eviction process, which took another seven months before I could regain my property and sell it. I maintain I have a good God, as in the circumstances I think most buyers would have been put off and sought another property. In my case the buyers were very supportive and waited patiently until they could buy the house. In the end I was able to sell my house like everyone else without aspersions to my character. This is probably due to the judge and court staff who were supportive and aware of the unfairness of the situation. I would just add that often, because the tenant wouldn't pay the rent or wouldn't pay the total amount of rent, I was often left in a precarious situation in terms of paying for accommodation. This was I believe a deliberate lack of concern for another human being, and I find it inconceivable that another person could have had such a total disregard for someone else's life and situation. In fact there were instances when I would have been homeless and without a place to sleep if it had not been for those who took me in when my situation was desperate.

I would like to pay a special tribute to all who took me in, regardless of the outcome, we may have fallen out, but this does not take away from my appreciation of what you did or tried to do for me. Thank you. I am aware that this includes some members of the metropolitan police who were aware of the situation and did their best to ensure I had somewhere to sleep.

The house was finally sold in July 2010, and I left for a holiday in America and then onto St Vincent ostensibly to get a new passport. I was to spend nearly eight months in St Vincent, and it was there that I learned many of the things which I have previously mentioned. While living in St Vincent & the Grenadines there was a political election which I found quite interesting as I have never witnessed the political process in the Caribbean. The music which accompanied the campaigns was very upbeat and ensured that you knew which party was delivering its speech. One particular song which was played regularly throughout the campaign was 'me and my neighbour voting for labour.' A very catchy song which to some extent captured the essence of the country. In December 2010 Dr. Hon. Ralph E Gonsalves was re-elected as Prime Minister of St Vincent and the Grenadines. A month earlier I was impressed at how people had reacted after a hurricane which had devastated much of the banana crop, and the sense of responsibility which every person adopted to ensure that roads and habitations were made safe. It was also sadly at this time that my late uncle's wife died.

I left St Vincent in May 2011 and returned to London, England where I sorted out my financial affairs which included closing an unsuitable bank account. Hopefully, my on-going financial transactions will not attract such negative comments and intrusive remarks about my anatomy and other inappropriate remarks.

Although I was not in London for the royal wedding on my return I was very aware of the previous celebrations which had taken place by the general public to mark the marriage of the second in line to the throne, Prince William and his new bride Kate. There was still a healthy ambience and feeling of goodwill which was evident within a few days of my arrival. In addition the street banners which marked the street parties were still in place. It was reminiscent of another royal wedding which had taken place some years before in 1981 that of Prince Charles and Princess Diana. I clearly remember attending the engagement celebrations in Hyde Park with Navaro. The atmosphere had been vibrant and there was a sense of having been part of a historic occasion. Later in July

2011, Zara Phillips, daughter of Princess Anne in a private ceremony married her partner with whom she had lived for many years.

On my return to England, I visited Leeds and met up with a few friends. I spent most of my time in London, and visited the theatre on several occasions as well as the cinema. I ensured I took in the sequel to *Phantom of the Opera*, entitled *Love never Dies* which was absolutely fantastic. I did not know anyone's voice could be so beautiful, and as the plot unfolded to the most beautiful arias I have ever heard I experienced real delight. I have made myself a promise that on my return to London I will take in another performance. My soul was truly lifted to heavenly heights and I knew moments of pure joy as the performance unfolded.

As I have previously mentioned I grew up in Leeds, but have spent most of my adult life in London, England. Primarily living in the north west of London, and later moving out to the suburbs in Harrow, Middlesex. The town of Harrow was once surrounded by green fields, similar to that of Wellingborough. Today it is more of an urban town with a diverse population consisting of people from the Caribbean, their offspring who are considered to be Black British, a large Asian population and of course English people. The famous Harrow on the Hill School is still educating young people, but does not seem as exclusive as it once was. Interestingly enough there are two famous people who attended this public school, the poet Byron and a previous Prime Minister of England, Winston Churchill.

Over the years I have watched pupils strikingly dressed in their uniforms coming and going to the school. There is definitely a sense of taking part in some momentous occasion when the school term begins. I have never taught in this academic climate, but feel a sense of reverence and even awe for those who have previously wandered along the school's corridors. As an educator I am also interested in the school's curriculum and the attainment of its students.

During my teaching career I have taught several Shakespeare plays, primarily at GCSE level, and I have selected two which I would like to briefly discuss as I believe they show parallels with my own situation at times. The plays that I would like to discuss in more depth are *As You like It* and *Hamlet*. Shakespeare's play *As You like It* considers man's capacity for change, and the varying factors which might influence those changes whereas *Hamlet* is a play which deals with revenge delayed. As I discuss the two plays mentioned I will also draw the necessary analogies with my own life experiences.

"This above all: to thine own self be true"[34]

In the play *Hamlet*, Prince Hamlet is accosted by his father King Hamlet's ghost which tells him that his brother, Claudius, who has since inherited the throne, was directly responsible for his death. The King was murdered by his brother who later marries his wife. King Hamlet tells his son that he must avenge his murder, but Prince Hamlet procrastinates. He needs the answers to many questions before he dare act. Some might argue that his unwillingness to act swiftly is to his advantage as it means he would be a fair and wise King when he ascends the throne. He would not simply accept someone else's word, but would test the spirit. In postponing his actions until he can prove the accuracy of the accusations he shows good judgement, although his behaviour seems erratic and somewhat aberrant to others.

Prince Hamlet ponders whether the ghost is a reliable witness, or is it really a misleading fiend. Is the ghost perhaps deluded? And how can it know for sure who killed him? He also asks how we can know the facts about a crime that has no witnesses. In his search for the truth the prince must certainly have seemed insane, yet in reality there is method in his madness.

> "In *Hamlet* the question of how to act is affected not only by rational considerations, such as the need for certainty, but also by emotional, ethical and psychological factors."[35]

Prince Hamlet successfully avenges his father by killing his uncle, and in turn is struck by a poisoned sword and eventually dies. Not however before his mother drinks the poison from the goblet. At the end of the play the whole royal family dies, and the throne is seized by a Norwegian Prince.

The parallels or similarities between the themes in the play, *'Hamlet'* and my own situation are I believe quite evident. The prince although he appears mad and dissembles, is actually quite sensible in searching for the truth before he acts. I believe I have been quite sensible, and have not simply accused anyone of wrongdoing. I have however as previously pointed out been accused of wrongdoing where there is no proof. Prince Hamlet is cautious as he is aware of the seriousness of killing his uncle, his mother's new husband. I would argue that the play isn't so much about indecisiveness, but more about a man's quest to understand and gain the truth. I believe my situation parallels, Prince Hamlet in my quest to understand the actions and motivations of those who knew the truth of my life.

Whereas *Hamlet* is a tragic play, which ends with the main protagonist's death, the play *'As You Like It'* is a comedy which promotes the view that man is capable of great change, and even sacrificial change if the need arose. Like the Holy Bible it discusses the stages of man from infancy into boyhood; and then from boyhood into manhood. In Act 2, Scene 7 of the play Jaques says:

"Man passes from infancy into boyhood, becomes a lover, a soldier, and a wise civic leader, and then, year by year, becomes a bit more foolish until he is returned to his second childishness and mere oblivion."[36]

Most of us go through these changes, and throughout my autobiography I have tried to illustrate my experiences in each of the stages. I have yet, I would argue to return to my second childhood, and am not yet at the stage of oblivion, but these things will eventually come to pass. I also selected this particular play because it deals with the theme of exile, and banishment. It is my contention that the difficulties I experienced in terms of selling my property are similar to those of the characters in the play who were forcibly removed or threatened from their homes.

At the end of the play there are four marriages, and a sense of a' utopian' world where the right things are done and everyone will live happily ever after. This is perhaps a little unrealistic; however the notion of restoration and healing is one which I would like to emulate in my own life. I believe that this has been achieved to some extent by moving from an oppressive and unhealthy environment into a new and refreshing experience which I believe offers more opportunities for self-exploration and development.

"All the world's a stage, and all the men and women merely players. They have their exits and their entrances. And one man in his time plays many parts "[37]

Essentially we play out our lives in a public arena, in the workplace, in social settings, and have our public as well as private personaes. We enter in at certain points in time and are engaged in certain aspects of life, and move on and change as we get older. We often play many roles, that of a child, teenager, adult and senior adult. We may also play the role of mother, daughter, employee, friend and lover.

Notes by the author or the Musings of a Nitwit
(the phrase was coined by someone else)

It's the 26th August 2011 and I made a voice recording of what I did today. When I replayed it a few days later I thought it might make interesting reading for anyone who might be going through the same process. I started writing about two weeks ago, and am continuing. The book hasn't taken shape, and I'm not using the correct grammar or vocabulary, I'm just making notes of what I want to say, I am becoming increasingly aware that I will have to re-organise the whole thing and put it in language which is more effective. At the moment it's not even like a diary account, it's very simplistic, not simply the style, but the language which is being used to recount the tale.

I also seem to have deviated somewhat from the original notes that I jotted down in a note book. The themes that I identified earlier (that is the seven deadly sins) no longer seem as applicable; although I am sure they will be mentioned when I consider the psychology of religion.

Currently my writing seems to be focusing on abuse, and if I think about it abuse is a central theme in my own life. This ranges from accusations of abuse from a distant cousin, to an awareness of abuse in other's lives, as well as my own. The book also seems to have become a biographical account, and I don't really want it to be my life story, although of course as the central protagonist, and omniscient narrator, I am the one who is re-counting the tale. It is very much from my perspective, however, I don't want it to be about ME, ME, ME or this happened to me and that happened to me, and essentially sounding as if I am full of woe. This is far from the truth, and I am blessed and really thankful for strength and life.

I think it will have to take another form. It needs to have other voices, and that's not coming through at the moment. So, as I said I'm very much making notes or writing about the things that have happened or my understanding of the things that have happened. I will then have to take it and re-shape it, maybe that's how it works, and I don't know I've never written before. I'm just going to persevere.

I'm enjoying what I'm doing, it's artistic, and appeals to the creative side of my personality.

Author

Notes by the author 27th August 2011

I spent most of the day very much as I said I would, in writing up my autobiography. It sounds very pretentious really doesn't it, but really it's not so much about me. Admittedly it's written in the first person and talks about my experiences, but I think if you look at it as a broader whole, it's about the experience of abuse it's not about Beverly Cuffy, per se. It's about the perceptions and the way someone is treated because of these perceptions. I think it's really important that it's documented.

As I wrote I was aware that I was not an isolated instance, and many have experienced abuse, either because they are different, physically or mentally challenged or unable to defend themselves for whatever reason. My acceptance of these things doesn't mean I think it's right just an awareness of the human condition. The nature of things is the survival of the fittest, and those who are not as fit may well be subject to bullying and or intimidation. My argument is that because I cannot hear sufficiently to defend myself, instead of family members being supportive they were critical and I suppose disappointed. This manifested itself in many ways.

There was I openly admit a time in my life when I needed the support of family members, and by this I don't mean by patronising me and telling me what to do, time to get up, get dressed, eat, go to bed, etc.; establishing a routine. That was and still is not necessary; anyone with common sense is able to establish a routine for themselves. However the support required was not forthcoming, and instead Lamp post made fun of me, and encouraged others to do the same. I am an intelligent woman, and if there is a difficulty quite capable of dealing with it, however I need to know about the matter in order to deal with it. Lamp post had a way of telling people to sshh! She doesn't want me to know.

My inability to hear everything has made life a little more difficult than when my hearing was good, and many have taken advantage of me because of it, and that in itself is very sad. I am not sad—I am sad because of the situation. I suppose I could witter on and on, but it would be to no avail.

On another note I wrote at length about Maestro. I had hoped to get some factual information, but without success. I will find out at some point, I will ask; but I suspect that what I think is the case is true. I don't have any dates or specifics, and out of sheer curiosity would like to have more accurate knowledge. It will not change anything, what's happened has already happened and we all have to live with the consequences of what we have done. I include myself in that comment, because I am neither perfect nor a saint, and I have at times acted in ways which were not suitable. However time moves on, days go by and life continues. Praise God.

The Author

References/Bibliography

Websites and Books

1. The Private Self (Theory and Practice of Women's Autobiographical Writings By Joanne Braxton (http://www.temple.edu/temptress/titles/439_reg.htm)

2. Peter Sutcliffe The Yorkshire Ripper (http://en.wikipedia.org/wiki/Peter_Sutcliffe)

3. *Wilt* by Tom Sharpe (h1ttp://en/wikipedia.org/wiki/Wilt)

4. 11th September 2001 Terrorist Attacks in America (http://en.wikipedia.org/wiki/September-11-attacks)

5. *Jane Eyre* by Charlotte Bronte (www.booksie.com/all/all/princess onika-auguste) Victorian Society's Interpretation of Madness (www.enotes.com/madness-nineteenth century literature)

6. Poem *Mental Cases* by Wilfred Owen (www.enoters.com/madness-nineteenthcentury Literature (http://www.europeanhistory.about.com/library/weeklyblowenme)

7. Short Story by Shirley Cooper *Shirley P Cooper* Published Harper Collins 1995 (http://www.redbubble.com/people/sisi)

8. Definition of flashbacks
(http//en.wikipedia.org/wiki/flashback_(psychology)

9. The Law and Defamation
(http://www.wisegeek.com/what is defamation of Character)

10. The novel *The Color Purple* by Alice Walker
(http://en.wikipedia.org/wiki/The Color Purple)
'*The Color Purple*' by Alice Walker
(http://www.library.csi.cuny.edu/dept/history/lavender/purple.html)

11. *I Know Why The Caged Bird* Sings by Maya Angelou
(http://www.sparknotes.com/lit/cagedbird/themes/html.)

12. Abuse A definition
(http://kidshealth.org/teen/yourmind/families/family_Abuse)

13. Black Politics of the 70s
(http://pubs.socialistreviewindex.org.uk/isj68/brown.htm)

14. *Men are from Mars, Women Are from Venus by John Gray*
(http://en.wikipedia.org/wiki/Men-Are-from-Mars,
    Women-Are-from-Venus)
(http://bible.org/article/men-are-mars-women-are-venus)

15. *The Holy Bible*(King James Ed.) Ephesians 5:22-31

16. *The Holy Bible* (King James Ed.) I Peter 3:7

17. Why do women stray from their partners
(www.psychology today.com/blog/women-who-stray
    (David J Ley PhD—Pub 2010)

17. Women's infidelity—'The only place where you'll find out
    the real reason women are cheating as much as men' by
    Michelle Langley
(http://women's infidelity.com)

18. Article entitled: "Think men are the unfaithful Sex? A
    study shows WOMEN are the biggest cheats—they're
    just better at lying about it by Maureen Rice
(http://www.dailymail/co.uk/femail/article-12111104/Think_m

19. Karl Marx's Theory on religion
(http://atheism.about.com/as/weeklyquotes/a/marx01.htm)

20. Allports view on religion
(http://psychology.wiki.com/wiki/psychology-of-religion)

21. The Holy Bible (King James Ed)Leviticus 19.31

22. The Holy Bible (King James Ed)1 Corinthians 13:11

23. William Wordsworth nature poet
(http://www.sol.com.au/kor/603.htm 1770-1850 19th Century Poet)

24. Songs of Innocence and Experience Shewing the two
    contrary states of the Human Soul—William Blake
(http://www.teachit.co.uk/armoore/poetry/blake.htm)

25. The Holy Bible (King James Ed) Matthew 5:48

26. Fromms view on religion
(http://en.wikipedia.org/wiki/Erich_Fromm)

27. Dysfunctional Relationships
(http://en.wikipedia.org/wiki/Dysfunctional_Families)

28. Holy Bible (King James Ed) Proverbs 9:8-9

29. Play *The Wild Duck by* Henrik Ibsen
(http://engliterarium.blogspot.com/2008/12/wild-duck symbol)

30. Human Rights Act 1998—The Right to Privacy—Article 8
(http://en.wikipedia.org/wiki/privacy-laws)

31. Holy Bible (KingJames Ed)James 4:13-15

32. Poem: *Half Past Two* by U A Fanthorpe
(http://www.wilmots.me.uk/phpBB3/viewtopic.php?t=57

33. *Romeo and Juliet* by William Shakespeare—"what's in a
    name . . ."

(http://www.enotes.com/shakespeare-quotes/what-name-t)

34. *Hamlet b*y William Shakespeare
(www.sparknotes.com/Shakespeare/Hamlet/Themes)

35. *Hamlet* by William Shakespeare
(http://www.sparknotes.com/Shakespeare/Hamlet/Themes)

36. *As You Like It* by William Shakespeare
(http://www.sparknotes.com/Shakespeare/asyoulikeit/Then)

37. *As You Like It* by William Shakespeare
(http://www.sparknotes.com/Shakespeare/asyoulikeit/Then)

INFORMATION ABOUT HELP WITH ABUSE CAN BE
FOUND ON THE WORLD WIDE WEB. I HAVE PROVIDED
A FEW ORGANISATIONS WHICH CAN BE CALLED IN
VARIOUS COUNTRIES.

<u>ENGLAND</u>

Child Abuse Hotline	0800 1111
The Samaritans (UK)	0845 790 9090
The Samaritans International Number	1 850 60 90 90
Prayer line (UCB)	0845 456 7729
MIND Information Line	0300 123 3393
Co-counselling International (UK) National contact person Sue Gray	+44 788 525 5188

<u>NORTH AMERICA</u>

National Domestic Violence Hotline	1-800-799-SAFE (7233)
Rape, Abuse and Incest National Network(RAINN)	1-800-656-HOPE(4673)
National Child Abuse Hotline	1-800-4-A-Child

National Prayer line	1-866-273-4444
Co-counselling International UK	1-206-284-0311

CANADA

Domestic Violence Hotline	1-800-363-9010
National Child Abuse Hotline	1-800-4-A-Child
Prayer line and prayer requests	1-800-947-5433
Co-counselling International (UK) National contact person	+1-905-853-2743

CARIBBEAN—VIRGIN ISLANDS

National Domestic Violence Hotline	1-800-799-SAFE (7233)/1-800-787-3244
Childline in Caribbean	131-800-4321
Prayer line (The national Suicide Prevention Lifeline)	1-800-273-TALK (8255)